Being
An Empath
Today

Monique Joiner Siedlak

Being an Empath Today© 2019 Monique Joiner Siedlak

ISBN: 978-1-950378-18-0

Publisher

Oshun Publications, LLC

Cover Design by MJS

Cover Image by Depositphotos.com

Logo Design by MJS

Logo Image by Pixabay.com

Sign up to the **Newsletter** and receive my **Free Yoga_for_Depression_eBook!**

mojosiedlak.com/self-help-and-yoga-newsletter

Books in the Series

Creative Visualization

Astral Projection for Beginners

Meditation for Beginners

Reiki for Beginners

Manifesting With the Law of Attraction

Stress Management

Time Bound: Setting Your Goals

Healing Animals with Reiki

A Great Offer

Want to learn about African Magic, Wicca, or even Reiki while cleaning your home, exercising, or driving to work? I know it's tough these days to simply find the time to relax and curl up with a good book. This is why I'm delighted to share that I have books available in audiobook format.

Best of all, you can get the audiobook version of this book or any other book by me for free as part of a 30-day Audible trial.

Members get free audiobooks every month and exclusive discounts. It's an excellent way to explore and determine if audiobook learning works for you.

If you're not satisfied, you can cancel anytime within the trial period. You won't be charged, and you can still keep your book. To choose your free audiobook, visit:

www.mojosiedlak.com/free-audiobooks

Table of Contents

Introduction

Do you have a history of being misunderstood or considered weak and fragile for being too sensitive? Well, you will find this book a useful guide as you embark on a journey to reveal your hidden potentials. If you're able to sense other people's moods and hidden intentions, sense and predict the good and the bad that is coming your way, all while being highly sensitive to environmental influences, there are good chances that you are an empath. However, empathy is a lot more than plain sensitivity. Being an empath means being intuitive, kind, and compassionate.

This book will open up the critical questions and provide useful guidelines that every empath needs to live a balanced, healthy life. To start, this book will open up the question of what it truly means to be an empath. By looking into the meaning from all aspects, acknowledging spiritual, scientific, and medical interpretations of empathy, you will learn how to observe your authentic traits with compassion, understanding, and acceptance.

Being an empath means being sensitive to a broad range of stimuli and energies. This book will break down the different types of empathy so that you can better understand yourself and your own sensitivities. With this knowledge, you will know which strategies to use to protect your energy and heal yourself from exhaustion and overwhelm.

Furthermore, this book will teach you how to grow, nurture, and leverage your empathic abilities. This way, you will actually embrace your gift and learn how to manage your talent in a manner that benefits both you and those around you. By understanding your physical, energetic, and spiritual sensitivities, you will become equipped with the right knowledge to adjust your lifestyle. To grow and succeed instead of spending the precious time of your life in seclusion and isolation.

With strategies provided to empower you and help you reach the position of control and authenticity, this book will enable you to emerge from the shadows and insecurities. You will learn how to use foods, exercise, and your own connection with nature to draw energy and power rather than give it away.

If you've just become aware of your unique abilities, this book will provide guidelines to awaken your potential in a way that is healthy and safe. You will learn how to navigate not only your physical sensitivities but also spiritual awakening. To mature into an authentic empath who has the full grasp of their skills and talents.

A healthy, happy empath is also the one who is surrounded by the right people and engaged in a loving, respectful relationship. In this book, you will find useful advice to turn what was once your insecurities into strengths that you can use to form meaningful relationships.

While reading this book, be sure to note and apply the given advice to start healing and empowering yourself right now. Make sure that you keep your mind open as you read this book, as learning and gaining true knowledge is the key to finding success and empowerment.

Chapter 1: What Is an Empath

Who are you as an empath, indeed? There are numerous ways in which humanity views Empaths and people who are sensitive more than others. In psychology, the term Highly Sensitive Person (HSP) is used to describe people who possess a high level of sensitivity to external stimuli (Aron & Aron, 1997). Similarly, the term Sensory Processing Sensitivity (SPS) in science describes the type of neurological sensitivity that makes you more receptive and responsive to the signals and stimuli from the environment. But do these terms describe Empaths fully and accurately? Indeed, empathy does include an increased level of sensitivity to different forms of energetic signals, but it doesn't end there. Empathy also consists of an increased level of responsiveness, and from a spiritual point of view, which will be the framework of this book. It involves an extensive relationship with the energy within and around you in its various forms. If you have spent your whole life asking what is it that makes you so sensitive. Why you've sense intense visualizations in forms of dreams or visions. Why are you so deeply sensitive to the nature around you, and why the pains and aches of others affect you so profoundly, a spiritual approach provides an in-depth perspective.

Many Empaths practice spirituality and spiritual healing, learning about human energy, and how its flow affects a person. Since you have a more profound connection with this world, the material doesn't attract you as much. You lean toward deeper meaning and spiritual connection in all aspects of life.

Many Empaths come from a history of depression and anxiety. Sadly, anxiety, depression, and self-esteem issues are conditions that many Empaths suffer from. The world, as it is today, prioritizes utility, materialism, and hedonism over spirituality, which doesn't align with an Empaths personality. As a result, an empath can feel profoundly isolated from people and the increased sensitivity to light, smells, colors, and noises also contribute to overload and overwhelm.

Experts in psychology consider Empaths to be highly sensitive individuals. They do behavioral tests to inspect the person's sensitivities and help them recover and adjust. Psychology views Empaths highly sensitive people, with sensitive brains that pick up on other people's moods, energy, as well as signals from the environment. Instead of saying empath, they use the word Highly Sensitive Person or HSP.

People who are practicing their empathic abilities within the frames of spiritual healing see the grave importance in the awareness of the emotion and how it truly affects our lives. For instance, they have the increased ability to identify which behaviors and feelings come from suppressed issues and memories that were never processed or with which the person hasn't been coping well. If you're able to detect such problems, you may yourself encounter several challenges. First, distinguishing another person's emotional issues from your own, and, second, learning how to control taking in these influences. Third, one of your challenges is also whether to communicate your insights to the person. An unaware empath might feel others insecurities or suppressed anger as their own or act submissive to accommodate the person's troubles. A helper-empath might feel as if they have to help this person overcome their issues even if they don't want help. An empowered empath will pick up on the condition but know how to filter out its influence on their own energy. While they might feel open and willing to help, they will only do that if the person has asked them to and if they seem eager to work on their own issues.

Clinical psychology understands Empaths as a specific group when it comes to temperament and personality traits. While the term empath isn't a clinical construct, it is often used to address the recovery of narcissistic abuse. In a nutshell, emotional empathy means to feel someone else's feelings and be affected by the person's energy. It is not the same as the ability to be compassionate, which is the ability that most people have.

Empaths are not only good observers of others' (and nature's) traits and energy cues but are physically and mentally affected by other's signals. An empath who is not aware of their traits might suffer from numerous physical illnesses as a result of this. The main health risk when it comes to unbalanced emotions is that the Empath's body and mind are alerted continuously. Whether it's noises from the environment, the overwhelming feeling from having to deal with others' manifested issues or receiving energetic signals from nature that they haven't learned how to interpret, the flood of stimuli regularly alerts the Empath's neurological system. Up until it is no longer able to find a balance on its own. Not only that, numerous illnesses can result from this state. In spite of that, recovery entails constant work to retrain your nervous system. To be able to respond appropriately, while replenishing your body from the inside out.

An empath has a high level of alignment with the feelings of those around them. This trait, while useful to provide an insight into the person's true feelings, can also fall hard on an empath. You may feel the emotions that don't root in your reality and feel like there is something wrong with you. Frequently having this experience can make you question your own judgment and mental health. It can also make you feel like you're suffering from issues that aren't your own.

Aside from being easily influenced by others' energy, both emotionally and physically, Empaths can have difficulty communicating their own needs. This is true for both physical and emotional needs. When the empath is unaware of their natural tendencies and hasn't yet learned the skill of filtering out the influences, they can easily, and unconsciously, exchange the energy around them. Without any conscious insight into their traits, the empath will be under the constant influence of surrounding energy. As a result, Empaths are more sensitive to trauma and more vulnerable to abuse.

Empaths often haven't received the needed amount of protection as children. Raising a sensitive child is different than usual. Children who are withdrawn, shy, and have experiences unlike other children of their age, need a different approach and more understanding from their parents. Most Empaths don't receive enough insight into their sensitivities as children and are observed as weak for their sensitivities. As their interests are a bit different than those of other children, parents often push empathic children to belong and act the same way as other children. Especially when those children would most rather keep to themselves and draw or play alone in nature.

Empaths who've had traumatic childhoods that included abandonment, neglect, abuse or were raised by emotionally unavailable parents, will not only have difficulty establishing self-esteem and confidence but also be more vulnerable to codependency. These Empaths, as children, had to accommodate their parents and adopt coping behaviors to receive love and affection. Or avoid abuse, are at a higher risk of developing depression and pursuing dysfunctional relationships in adulthood.

Unconsciously, many people, empathic or not, seek the type of a person as a friend or a romantic partner who is similar to the partner whose approval and acceptance they didn't receive. The greater the trauma is, the greater the desire to please an abusive type of personality.

Regardless of their upbringing, Empaths absorb the energy of others and have difficulty in addressing their own needs. What is especially dangerous for Empaths is that they will quickly give up their energy to gain protection and support. This puts an empath into an interdependent state, where they will deny their vulnerability and try to please a person until they become completely exhausted.

Chapter 2: Types of Empaths

Empathy, observed as the quality of increased sensitivity and responsiveness, can be broken down into multiple groups of types. Psychologists often refer to the three main types of Empaths, but not based on their abilities, but rather the stages of maturity and personal development. While there are other types of empathy, you can look into to identify your own gifts. Looking into these three types is useful to pinpoint your current emotional state. What you can achieve to empower yourself and evolve. Keep in mind that while there are distinct categories, it is a continuum that can change. Meaning, you can move anywhere between these main types depending on your current emotional state.

The Authentic Altruist

This category is considered to be the healthiest, as the authentic altruist has matured both physically and emotionally. An authentic altruist is highly self-aware of their motivations, limitations, and the freedom of choice. Anywhere you look to learn about how to stay healthy empath, you'll discover that establishing and owning your decision to give or not give is crucial for an empath. An authentic altruist has recognized that giving and helping is a choice that you can make or not make.

Furthermore, this choice is unconditional, and it doesn't say anything about you and your personality. If you choose to set boundaries, the decision is your own, and you don't think of yourself as an evil, selfish person for not wanting to give. An authentic altruist understands that there's no use of helping prematurely to someone who is not willing to help themselves.

As you examine further into this book, you will learn just how important it is that you invest your energy, efforts, and resources only into those people who are open to receiving help. Those who are willing to help themselves. Neglecting to make this choice leaves many Empaths drained continuously, as they devote themselves to all the wrong people.

An authentic altruist understands that the act of giving is free and that giving and healing is in God's hands, not in theirs. This empath acknowledges their own right not to help or be there for anyone who reaches out to them. They don't place themselves at the center of the giving process. They are aware of their dark side (flawed, human nature, negative feelings). Being open to acknowledge and accept their shadow self helps them to reach authenticity. This shadow self is a collection of features and qualities that all humans share that are considered dark and negative. For an empath who struggles with self-image, boundaries, and feeling of obligation do give selflessly. Achieving authenticity often entails a lot of work both in terms of spiritual growth and talk therapy. These untruthful assumptions keep and empath trapped in a cycle of codependency with their environment. They also keep them in fear that if they stop giving, they will lose their life's purpose. Technically speaking, this empath is stuck between a rock and a hard place. On the one hand, giving selflessly to the wrong people, which is draining and toxic, and on the other, the prospect of losing the relationships they already have if they decide to "cut the cord" and establish boundaries, fills them with fear. Once an empath overcomes this fear and realizes that there's nothing that keeps them obliged to give themselves to others, they will become empowered and authentic in their altruism.

The Proud Helper

Most Empaths who haven't reached the level of authenticity fall into this category. It is not the best place to be in, but it is not as toxic and dangerous as being entirely dependent. The proud helper is on the path of setting themselves up for codependency. They are giving, generous, and have the capacity for both growth and failure. Unlike the philanthropist, who recognizes that they are helping for the sake of the other individual, the proud helper sees themselves as the focus of the act of giving. Often unintentionally, the proud helper gives to others what they desire to enhance their own self-image. They are not well aware of the importance of choice, and they engage in self-deception that prevents them from pulling back and making smart choices. They haven't yet become a self-destructive empath, but their potential for pride has the potential to harm them. A proud helper will secretly become resentful when their help is not appreciated or acknowledged. They can also become passive-aggressive. While a proud helper has a moderate level of mental awareness, and the ability to read the signals coming from the others and the environment, they are yet to establish the power and control over their capacity to give.

The Codependent Empath

The codependent empath expresses a high level of insecurity and dependence in their relationships. They not only can act self-destructive, but they might be continuously draining their bodies and minds to help others. A codependent empath is the most prone to unhealthy relationships. They have a pathological need to heal, save, and rescue a specific person who either manipulates them or doesn't want/ accept help. For a codependent empath, pursuing an emotionally unavailable person is an obsessive quality. It focuses on one specific person, most often emotionally, not only emotionally unavailable but often narcissistic or self-destructive. A codependent empath will get involved in a dysfunctional relationship to help save an abusive person, which results in harm to their own health.

It is an addictive, compulsive quality to find and heal people who look like they need help, but don't accept it. A codependent can fear abandonment. They may become violent and have physical and psychosomatic illnesses as a result of a toxic relationship. The psychological profile of a codependent is such that they come from a place of insufficient self-esteem, and use their helpful intentions as a way of getting love, appreciation, acknowledgment, and acceptance. Since they focus on other people to obtain what they, essentially, need to give to themselves, their efforts are in vain, and they become trapped in ever-growing need to please. As a result of negative experiences and lack of reward for their kindness and support, a codependent can view the world as an evil place. To them, they are victimized and unappreciated.

Aside from the level of personal development, Empaths can differ depending on the type of sensitivity that they have. Not all Empaths are sensitive to people's feelings. Some are sensitive to other stimuli, like those coming from nature, plant and animal world, as well as the different planes of existence.

Plant Empaths

You can communicate with the plants. You might turn to them when you are upset. You like to touch them, and you feel like they can hear you. Plants flourish around you. Plant Empaths enjoy gardening and fieldwork. You need to be near the natural world to feel healthy and happy. Plant homeopathy might help you heal your ailments and feel in tune with the natural world. You can receive the guides from plants. You also feel the sadness of plants being destroyed.

Earth Empaths

You attune with the earth and are sensitive to its changes. It nourishes and sustains you, and you are sensitive to the weather. The earth elements feel like family. You feel the connection with the earth and your body is intimately connected with it. You may feel hurt and anxious when the Earth is harmed. You will have to learn how to navigate the body's responses and practice self-care when the changes occur. Hurricanes, eruptions, and earthquakes happen near intense solar activity, and you can sense that, responding with anxiety and depression. When the sun goes through changes, so do you. You need to frequently connect with the Earth and deepen your bond by eating clean and healthy. Junk foods separate you from the Earth. Walking barefoot is also helpful. Be open to the intuitions that come. Earth answers and you should follow her guidance. You can practice earth medicine by cherishing the planet.

Animal Empaths

You can communicate with animals, and you can understand how animals feel. You attract animals wherever you go. You also benefit from working with animals. Some saints were able to talk to animals. Introverted Empaths like seclusion with animals only and feel the need to be of service to animals. Your pets know when you are in pain and respond with unconditional love. You may be able to sense what the animals are thinking. Animal medicine provides healing from animals, and you gain it from interacting with animals.

Meditation to call on the power of animals can protect you. Jaguar is a guardian that helps keep the negative energy away. Its energy enables you to center yourself and let go of stress. It circles your energy field and keeps the negative forces out. Give inner thanks when finishing the meditation. You can also call out to other animals you resonate with.

Intuitive Empaths benefit from divine interventions. Also, make sure to protect yourself from the inherent overload. You have to learn how to shut it off. Pace yourself to stay grounded.

Emotional Empaths

Empaths can sense how a person is feeling at the current time, in all the complexities of emotion. Empathy is present in most people to a certain degree. Most people can observe how the other person is feeling, which, in return, causes them to feel a certain amount of the same feeling. Unlike the natural ability to sense a person's current mood, Empaths can feel the genuine emotions that the other person is feeling like their own feelings. Empaths possess the awareness of a higher degree when it comes to feelings. If you are an empath, your ability to sense how the other person is feeling spreads beyond what meets the eye. You are capable of detecting underlying emotional issues, like fear, anger, or anxiety. You are also able to identify kindness and love even when people aren't keen to show them. This makes you a good friend to those who are sensitive on the outside, yet hard and cold-looking on the outside.

Whichever the type of an empath you may be, there are a certain number of personality traits that are common to most Empaths. The following sections will further explain these personality traits, as well as provide useful strategies to navigate their positives and negatives.

Chapter 3: Personality Characteristics That Most Empaths Represent

Numerous signs point to the possibility that one is an empath. From early childhood to adulthood, Empaths often get confused with merely being introverted. As a result, Empaths suffer a lot of isolation as a judgment. Often considered to be just too sensitive, they are told to "toughen up," and they end up suppressing their gifts and unique abilities. This chapter will further explore the specific traits of Empaths that distinguish them from other people.

Are All Empaths Introverts?

While some Empaths are introverts, not all of them are. Similarly to introverts, you're prone to feeling overwhelmed and drained after spending a lot of time in crowded spaces or surrounded by loud noises. Empaths are sensitive to numerous types of energies and can get easily overstimulated. Because Empaths respond to enormous amounts of stimuli on a daily level, sudden and frequent mood swings can occur. It is your natural ability to take in the mood of another person. Just as well as to quickly pick up both the positive and the negative of your work environment. It can cause your moods to vary along with these energies.

People-Readers

You can tell if someone is lying and you're good at reading people. An upside of this is that you can easily detect any deceptions, while the downside is that you can become suspicious of people depending on your sensitivities. You can't stand disagreement, and you likely give a lot of your energy into maintaining a peaceful environment. While this can be beneficial on some levels, in the long run, you may be prone to ignoring problems that need to be addressed. Opposite to that is the need to solve issues immediately, even when it's too soon to address them, or the person isn't ready to confront a particular problem.

Sensitive to Violence

Most Empaths are susceptible to violence in the media. As the news and the media articles become increasingly sensationalist in modern society, the overwhelm of great daily news might disturb you. They might hear about a tragedy which isn't related to their community and is struck by grief or anger for days.

Depending on your other personality traits, you might be quirky and creative. Inspiration and creativity go hand-in-hand with empathy. You can inspire after and understand emotions, as well as to picture them vividly.

Eclectic Taste and Open-Mindedness

Most Empaths are open-minded, or at least more so than an average person. Rather than choosing to stay in your comfort zone, you like to explore different concepts and philosophies both in terms of spirituality and creativity. Your choices vary based on moods rather than style, which often results in an eclectic taste. Your style might be a blend of old and new, and you love to explore different options when it comes to clothing and interiors.

Daydreamers

Empaths are devoted friends and good listeners. While you're good at engaging in meaningful conversations, you can easily drift off into your fantasies if the topic doesn't hold your attention. You don't enjoy small talk and shallow conversations. If you can't get out of a conversation that doesn't interest you, you might retreat to the inner world of fantasy.

The Need for Seclusion

You require more alone time than most individuals because your emotional life can be exhausting and overwhelming. The physical stimuli can contribute to the feeling of overwhelm. You need solitude to regain strength, focus, and a sense of balance. You relax by being on your own and engaging in calming, creative activities. Chances are you enjoy craftwork, artwork, meditation, spiritual practices, and other things that help you unwind and regain energy.

Hyperactivated Attachment System

You seek connection and intimacy more than an average person. This form of a hyperactivated attachment system affects how you form bonds with parents and romantic partners. It is also responsible for more intense feelings of warmth and intimacy than typical in most people. Your attachment trigger is easily switched on, and you find it easier to feel kindness, sympathy, and empathy. In fact, there is so much of it that you start wanting to give to others and connect. When this desire is highlighted, it can create a lot of problems. Empaths can be easily influenced by others' energy and energy frequencies. Hyperactivate attachment is responsible for your intuitive nature, but it can have a harmful impact when there are insufficient self-esteem and autonomy. Combined with an increased tendency to bond, the lack of self-confidence can result in unhealthy attachment and toxic relationships.

Most Empaths find joy in pleasing others. When this tendency becomes a need, due to attachment issues, Empaths can become overly people-pleasing without sufficient regard to their own needs.

While these are the most distinct personality traits of Empaths, they possess more profound, unique qualities that don't meet the eye. The following sections of this chapter will further elaborate the most prominent characteristics of an empathic personality.

An Excellent Intuition

If you're an empath, you are highly intuitive. To truly understand and interpret your intuitive signs correctly, you need to learn how to distinguish it from fears and desires. Sometimes, what you think to be your "gut feeling" isn't your intuition at all. When you're highly intuitive, you have an increased sense and the ability to understand others' emotions. You might also be good at "reading" people. Your sensory perception is heightened, and others' energy can affect that perception. You're a sharp observer of people surrounding you, including both the positive and negative human traits.

Not all Empaths are equally intuitive, but they are more intuitive than the general population. It is additionally essential to note that because a person is intuitive, it doesn't have to mean that they are automatically empathetic. Your inherent nature allows you to understand and evaluate a situation while taking in the stimuli from the outside world. Combined with empathy, intuition creates a unique gift. When your intuition is heightened, you will be extra sensitive to representations of pain and distress. You may be affected by news or the sights of people and animals suffering.

As an empath, your intuition is beyond what psychologists call a "highly sensitive person." You are capable of receiving the information that defies the logical. With the strengthening of your abilities, your awareness also grows. You might be experiencing intense visions and dreams and even communicate with animals. Science doesn't yet understand all of the properties that Empaths possess and being unable to explain your abilities might make you feel lonely and isolated. You should try to stay grounded and learn how to interpret your experiences in a balanced, centered way. It is all right to follow your intuition and allow it to guide your life. You are also sensitive to elements. You can sense the energy around people, and often detect people's illnesses, even death. Being unable to talk about these experiences and other people not understanding your abilities can cause isolation. On the other hand, being unable to understand your own experiences can bring a lot of shame, sadness, and anxiety. Your sensitivity simply allows you to pick up on subtle cues most people aren't able to.

You may identify with many types of empathic abilities. Whether or not you believe that your intuition comes from the inborn ability or the supernatural, it is how you navigate it that matters.

Exploring a Spiritual Connection

While most Empaths share a connection to the world around them, some are sensitive to the links that aren't physical, but somewhat spiritual.

Telepathic Empaths

Telepathic Empaths receive mental signals from others. For example, you can sense that a loved one is in distress even if you're far away. You must get to know yourself well and learn how not to project your fears onto your perceptions of the intuition. You might have an unconscious fear and project that fear into the feeling that something terrible will happen. You can also experience the overload of telepathic information before you learn to filter out with grounding and shielding. Still, when there's room to help you should do so.

Mediums

You may receive information about the future about different areas of your life. This is called non-local information. You reach beyond linear reality. The knowledge of precognitive ranges back to ancient cultures. Keep in mind that what you are sensing is only a probability, and there is always the possibility of being wrong. Consistently think about whether the information is appropriate to share and whether it is helpful. Does the time feel right? You have many misconceptions about your gift. You don't have to get involved with the events, nor are you causing them.

Strong, Lucid Dreams

You have, and you also remember, experiencing very vivid dreams. They bypass the ego and the mind to offer intuitive information. These dreams describe you how to help yourself and others. You are very in sync with dreams and so are also tuned in with other people. They can tell you how to overcome the obstacle. If you feel like you have a spirit guide, be sure to listen. You can develop your abilities by keeping a journal and record whatever you remember about your dreams. There are numerous ways you can take in interpreting your dreams. Learning from your dreams helps you understand yourself and others. In lucid dreams, you can direct the outcome of the dream.

Spiritual Development

Empaths may have a different degree of ability to communicate with the other side and bridge the gap beyond the material plane. You allow the intuitive messages to come through. You can develop these skills with proper guidance. Certain mediums channel angels. Mediums have existed throughout the centuries. One of the ways to practice your skills is to identify the person you want to reach and ask to contact them. This person is pure energy, and connecting can feel replenishing, but also overwhelming. This can take place spontaneously to untrained people. You have the right to declare no to any experience you don't call for. As you practice, you will feel more comfortable setting boundaries. You can look at your abilities in a new way to thrive in the world. You are a visionary, a compassionate, and spiritual-oriented in the world that can be very hard and ruthless. Whichever your place of work might be, there are ways in which the work team can benefit from your unique contribution. You can develop empathic abilities to find success. It is a big gift that comes with a lot of responsibility.

Susceptible to the Emotional Moods of Other Individuals

You are also prone to help others solve their conflicts and act as intermediate. You see yourself as a peacemaker, and you enjoy helping people reduce stress and resolve their own issues. While this is an extraordinary trait, make sure to not go to absolute avoidance of conflict on the one side or extreme meddling into other people's problems on the other.

You are patient and calm when making decisions because you feel the need to make sure that the choices are not being influenced in any way. Being patient in your position is wise, considering the probability of misinterpreting emotional and visual cues. To sharpen your instincts, work toward learning to distinguish intuition from inner fears, desires, and emotional issues.

You can understand and feel the emotions of loved ones even when they're not with you. This can lead to feeling strange and sudden feelings of both negative and positive nature only to learn that a loved one felt that way at the same time.

Sensing Distress in Crowded Areas

You might have difficulty coping with crowds and find it hard to understand why people enjoy it. Being forcefully in groups can make you feel ungrounded. You can become grounded when you are in your element. Exercise and yoga are helpful to feel good in your body, but you need to figure out your personal issues to actually enjoy being grounded. Self-confidence is the key to being grounded.

Anxiety can happen without any reason and has to do with vague fears and worries. It has to do with the lack of faith, which is why the medication often doesn't help. You need to understand whether or not this anxiety is genuinely coming from you. You are often worried about others, but excessive worrying can harm the person you are concerned about. Don't ask to fix someone who didn't ask for help. If someone needs help, they will ask for it. When you don't know and can't interpret these cues, you might take it as your own. Then, you can lose the ability to focus on yourself. Vocalize the need for support, but no one can solve other people's issues. People need to handle their own problems to learn and grow. You have to learn how to say no and learn how to put your concerns and recovery first. You are extra sensitive to shame and guilt.

You want to avoid the energy vampires; particularly those who are making you feel guilty. You may feel anxious, but unable to tell why. This is for the lack of faith that everything will work out.

Sensing the Room

Unlike most people, you will pick up on the subtle energies and the dynamics of the group. You feel the vibe of the room and the energy of the people in it. If you detect an environment to be hostile or unfriendly, you might suddenly decide to leave. While this may come off as unusual to other people, you should trust your instinct and not force yourself to be in a non-friendly environment. However, in the long run, you should work toward strengthening your ability to filter out those influences and be able to partake in different settings. While your sensitivity isn't bad in any way, having to retreat every time and with any group that doesn't feel supportive isn't a good solution either. Your goal should be to strengthen and affect other energies with yours in a positive way, not to back out.

This chapter examined the distinct features of an empath that set them apart from the average people. These features direct how you create relationships and view yourself. While your strongest empathic personality traits may, at times, make your life hard, you should consider them as gifts rather than as a burden. This chapter looked into some of the main Empaths' personality traits. The following chapters will examine the different aspects of an Empath's life, and provide useful advice to turn, what you once thought to be weaknesses into strengths.

Chapter 4: How to Embrace Your Ability

Becoming an empowered empath should be your primary goal when reading this book, and when working toward improving your life and abilities. Many Empaths come from a history of under nurtured potential. Combine this with life-long exposure to stressful influences, may result in self-doubt, sense of not-belonging, and overall detriment to one's wellbeing.

Being an empath is profoundly rewarding, once you learn how to empower yourself, and center your energy and thoughts. This chapter will further elaborate on the process of embracing your abilities.

The Importance of Embracing Versus Suppressing Your Gift

As an empath, you can experience a profound passion and joy and have the capacity to help others. Your sensitivity makes you caring and loving. You are drawn to the natural world, and you feel the need to connect to it. You like to feel at one with nature. You have the power to change yourself to empower yourself and surpass negativity positively. You can be in control and able to heal yourself. You can detach from abuse and neglect through the acceptance of your gifts. The more you are aware of your abilities, the more you can change and grow.

The Power of Vulnerability

Compassion is your biggest strength because it guides healing and understanding. But, the fear can block your way into the light. Vulnerability is another one of your strengths, and the path to peace in your life, along with the spiritual work. You are contributing to improving the world with compassion and healing. You dare to make the world more humane in a corporate, non-sensitive world. If you stay centered and open, you can contribute to the improvement of the world around you. The more confident you are, the better you can clarify how your empathy can contribute to the world.

The Importance of Self-Reflection

Self-reflection helps you embrace your empathy. You can tune into your intuition and find the best choices. When you are afraid and don't know what to do, you will find the answer by showing compassion and empathy toward yourself. Acceptance and exercise position you as an empowered empath versus the one who is influenced by others. When embracing your empathic abilities, keep in mind that you are not alone. Other positive and sensitive people can amplify their powers. The community will enforce you and replenish your energy with the positive.

Embrace Your Community

Since life can feel so overwhelming, you might give in to stress. You can learn the strategies to shelter yourself from the overload. While you may be a loner, you benefit from the community that leans toward the meaningful. On the other hand, isolation might be toxic to you as you need a connection with other people. You need to experience love and feel like you are contributing to the world to feel well.

Embrace Empathy with Self-Love and Gratitude

Each morning, make sure to ground yourself and practice the techniques of self-love, gratitude, and journaling to sharpen your intuition and tune into the positive energy of the environment. Gratitude, as in being grateful for your progress and compassion when you are not doing well, is the way to go to empower yourself as a natural empath. Your sensitivities and the kind heart can help you bond with other Empaths to empower each other. Honor your sensitivities all the way through. Use your intuition to better yourself as much as the rest of the world. You have numerous tools available to shelter yourself from negativity, stress, and overload. This places you in a state of balance.

Practice Meditation and Shielding

Meditation helps you relax and tune into your actual positive energy. Shielding allows you to become resilient to all sorts of uninvited stimuli and establish control over when you will open up and when you won't. Eating healthy and clean helps you stay in tune with the powerful energy of the Earth and the plant world. Staying connected, both with humans and animals, help you stay grounded and loved. It creates a circle of giving and receiving compassion and love.

Process, Don't Suppress

Your goal is to learn how to process your feelings, not prevent them or to reduce them. On the one hand, trying to train yourself somehow to reduce the number of feelings that come your way is useless because it goes completely against your nature. On the other hand, ignoring or suppressing your emotions, which are all forms of avoidance, one of the most dysfunctional coping mechanisms, may lead to all sorts of psychosomatic symptoms. Unless you learn how to process your feelings and establish continuous energetic boundaries to internalizing the emotions of others, any tactics or remedies used will only temporarily relieve your symptoms.

Being a highly sensitive person doesn't imply that you will continually have highly alerting emotions coming your way. It merely means that you have the potential to receive, but not the duty.

Be Kind to Yourself!

Understanding your potential to heal and help may make you feel inclined to do so. Even though your best efforts keep the desire under control, you may be overly self-judgmental in all aspects of life. Many factors work against an empath truly embracing yourself. An influential inner critic you adopted as a child when your needs weren't adequately met, and exaggerated expectations you place upon yourself after revealing your true potentials (both in terms of empathy and other, instrumental abilities), can cause profoundly loud negative self-talk that prevents you from loving yourself unconditionally. For an empath, the importance of unconditional self-love and self-acceptance is even higher than for a non-empath. Why? It is because the human brain is made to reflect what we feel for ourselves onto the exterior world. Those who are angry at themselves become angry at others, and those who deep down don't love themselves can't truly love others.

If you judge yourself too hard, it can only make things more difficult for you. Understand that it is impossible to meet the expectations of perfection because your "inner critic's" role is to make you feel unworthy always. Help one person, and the inner critic will tell you that you should have helped that family. Help their family, and the inner critic will tell you that you made the mistake of neglecting your own family along the way. There's no way you can win the inner critic! For that reason, nurturing unconditional self-love, unconditional self-acceptance, and strengthening your self-esteem are the path to overcoming internal criticism and anxiety.

Embracing your empathic gift means going from the position of submission and exposure to autonomy, altruism, and empowerment. Embracing empathy means accepting your inborn traits with gratitude rather than blocking and ignoring them. Empowering yourself as an empath means learning how to be in control of your potential to give and receive without feeling obliged to do so.

This chapter provided insight into the basics of embracing your empath lifestyle, while the following chapters will further break down the improvements that you can start making now to feel better and sharpen your skills.

Never allow the "inner critic" to make your feel bad about little details that DON'T MATTER. Silence the "inner critic".

Chapter 5: How Emotions and Empaths Work Together

Empaths have a complicated relationship with emotions, regardless of the nature of their sensitivity. This chapter will provide a glimpse into the background of the Empath's emotional struggles, as well as suggest the strategies for one to overcome the emotional fragility to move toward maturation and autonomy.

Empaths have a porous psychological structure, meaning that they lack the natural defense mechanisms that most people have. Due to many factors, an empath can be stuck in a pseudo-adult state. This is a state where they've reached physical and mental maturity, but not the emotional. Due to disturbances to their emotional development that were previously described, Empaths may not have developed the level of awareness, confidence, and autonomy of a mature adult. They can be hyper-agreeable and have trouble holding their ground.

They will quickly give up their power in exchange for security, acceptance, love, or lessening of the conflict.

Vulnerable To Emotional Abuse

Empaths are particularly vulnerable to narcissists. Their nervous system is more prone to constant stress and overwhelm. As they often feel overwhelmed by stimuli, Empaths have difficulty functioning under stress. If they encounter narcissists, Empaths can experience headaches or dissociation. If an empath has been under the continuous toxic influence by an energetic vampire for a long time, it will take a lot of work for them to heal. The greatest obstacle for an empath to heal in this situation is their struggle to regain the sense of inborn right to existence, love, and health. When an Empath's confidence has been diminished under the influence of a toxic person, they may start to feel like they always have to meet a specific set of criteria to consider themselves worthy.

Four States Of the "Self" (Self-Modes) Of Empaths

Self-states, or modes, are the parts of the psyche of every person that function separately. While being in one state, you are absorbing the mental traits of the environment, such as thoughts and emotions, and how you see the world. The self-states aren't separate personalities, but somewhat different aspects of the personality. Most people resort to a particular aspect of the personality that is desirable and helpful in a situation. As long as you are accessing all of your aspects in a balanced way, it can be considered a healthy way of living.

The trouble can happen when one becomes stuck in a particular mental state, and when it starts to shape how they see the world. To clarify, most of us show different aspects of the personality at work, at home, with friends and family, and in distress. A person can't behave the same way in all circumstances. For example, you might be harboring some anger and frustration at work, but you can release these feelings when you're alone at how or with your friends. If you start neglecting a particular aspect of your personality, suppression happens, and you aren't fulfilling all of your needs. If you, for example, allow your "office" self to dominate, you may take up on a cold, corporate view of the world. This can isolate you from friends and family and keep you from fulfilling your needs for connection, help, and support. Modes of the "self" boil down to different parts we are showing depending on what we find useful in a situation.

An Empath's psyche has four different states or modes. These modes require balancing for a person to feel calm and well. Out of the four primary modes, the two have matured, and the two haven't. Empaths often have the following self-states: the inner child, the inner critic, the adult, and the warrior. Please, keep in mind that these constructs were given names that somewhat accurately depict their roles. These aren't different personalities living within you, but aspects of you that take up diverse duties and store different types of experiences.

The Inner Child

The inner child is the most vulnerable aspect of your personality. It is considered to be the purest form of oneself. The Inner Child hasn't yet been shaped by the influences of the environment. Throughout the person's life, and during the process of maturation, the inner child readily receives the impressions of the environment. The inner child has the core needs for love and a sense of security. Since no one grows up with perfect parents/family, the inner child sacrifices the aspects of the true self to adapt and be able to gain love. When there's a considerable amount of adaptation or behavior based on early lack of love, security, and acceptance, the psychological issues can occur.

The inner child aspect of the Empath's personality has been overly developed. While this isn't bad in itself, having our most pristine, pure nature so close to the surface also activates other aspects of the personality to shelter it. This can create inner conflicts. The pure, untainted view of the inner child; the self is untouched by the world and hasn't been affected by environmental trauma. As a result, it hasn't been altered by environmental experiences and the adaptations of the ego. It is the source of life, luminous, and the inner nature of the human being. It is also most vulnerable to trauma.

The Critic

The inner critic is overly accessed by the empath. As a result of the Empath's inborn increased sensitivity, the inner critic has overdeveloped as a survival adaptation. As a child who was more sensitive from the get-go, you have developed healthy adaptations to gain love and care. The inner critic is a source of perfectionism, nihilism, skepticism, and criticism. This aspect of your personality has internalized the negative image of yourself that you've picked up while you were growing up. The inner critic is making you feel like you are not good enough and unworthy of the good in life unless it is deserved. The inner critic lacks the spiritual insight of the inner child. A strong inner critic is harmful due to the malicious nature with which it metaphorically attacks the inner child. What does this mean? Your inner critic is steadily reminding you of why are not good enough. It pops into your mind in the form of thoughts that are making you feel bad about yourself.

The Adult

The adult self-state is the healthiest form, as it guards and protects the inner child. The adult self-absorbs the attacks of the inner critic and can use the accurate, current data that hasn't been distorted by the extreme self-criticism. To simplify, the adult responds to the critic's unreasonable criticism with augmented, balanced knowledge. This way, it protects the inner child. The adult is capable of coping and taking responsibility for its actions. It is capable of thinking abstractly and evaluating one's own mental state.

The Warrior

The "warrior" is the full maturation of the adult who serves to protect both the adult and the inner child. It is incredibly protective and underdeveloped. Its role is to guard the pure nature of the inner child so that it isn't traumatized by the critic. It is triggered by the perceived injustice. You will know you have a warrior activated in moments when you become more aggressive in protecting yourself and when you stand up for yourself. The warrior is also self-aware and measured, but less than the adult. While the adult is the healthiest mode, circumstances indeed may entail for a more aggressive approach. There are many situations in which an adult approach to the matter won't yield results. When someone is openly trying to harm or offend you, or even physically and emotionally hurt you, it could happen that your version of an adult hasn't developed sufficient skills to cope. This is when the warrior kicks in as a result. Indeed, some situations can be extreme, and we can argue that there are certain situations when there's little choice. But, teaching your adult how to cope with these situations is necessary because aggressive responses aren't functional in the long run.

Strong Internal Critic

You can picture an internal critic as a psychological judge, who is continuously keeping tabs on your actions and makes you question them. While everyone has the internal critic, and it has a useful role in a person's mind, the distortion of this critic can become profoundly self-destructive. Your critic, or internal judge, can become distorted due to childhood trauma and insufficient acceptance in childhood. As a result of these, you may be unable to satisfy your inner criteria for success or self-worth, as the demands are ever-increasing.

Your inner judge, if overly empowered, will continuously whisper in your ear. It will let you know why every single thing you do isn't good enough. Perfectionism is a common trait of an empath, as we mentioned earlier. Since there's no perfection in the world or in life, you have to grow accustomed to being satisfied doing the best you can. An influential inner critic will always beat you up over missing the opportunity to perfect either your work, your life, or yourself. One of the ways to confront and weaken the inner critic as an empath is to stop fighting it. You must refuse to play by its rules. As with other things mentioned earlier, love and compassion are your main strengths. When you come across self-condemning thoughts, the best means to relieve them is to care for yourself with the same extent of love and compassion you would give to others. Respond to your critic with self-loving thoughts and confidence instead of struggling to push through and force self-confidence. By attacking the critic, you are merely giving it more strength.

Mastering Your Emotions as a Highly Sensitive Person

Being a highly sensitive person can become an asset, rather than being an obstacle. Learning how to navigate your sensitivities can help you thrive in all aspects of life.

While no schools of psychology acknowledge empathy, the term Highly Sensitive person is used to describe those whose neurological system is more sensitive, responsive, and vulnerable. There are many definitions of highly sensitive people. Many signs might indicate that you are a highly sensitive person, and it is necessary for you to know how to distinguish these terms to avoid misinterpretation.

Understanding the term empath correctly, in all its complexities, will help you to understand yourself better. It will help you know that the sensitivity isn't right or wrong, or good or bad. It just is, and the impact it has on your life and health is something that is up to you to navigate. The most straightforward formula might be to reduce the negative influence and enhance the positives. To further break things down for yourself, you can list all the pluses and minuses to having a clear picture of what you require to recover and flourish.

Compassionate and Understanding

On the bright side of being an empath is that you are a lot more compassionate to other people and more open to understanding others' feelings. It is a rare quality in the modern world where people worldwide suffer from anxiety and depression due to intense stress and the lack of understanding of the environment for their pain. It might come as a blow to you, but most people don't encounter understanding when they open up about their problems. Those who should be listening, in fact, often choose to judge or suggest premature solutions. They would instead embrace a hurting person with all of their sensitivities, flaws, and virtues and just be there for them. You have that rare talent, and even if you don't do anything more than that, you are a valuable friend, family member, and a coworker.

The Harmful Self-Neglect

One of the biggest mistakes that empathetic people make is that they don't give themselves sufficient attention and self-care. Empaths often feel obliged to help others, but they don't put enough work to help themselves and nurture themselves to stay healthy. Prioritizing oneself is difficult for an empath because they have a tendency to be selfless. As a result of this, you might be sacrificing your sleep, eating insufficiently, and failing to address your own issues. You don't find enough time for yourself, and the self-neglect quickly causes the weakening of the immune system, which by itself is a potential for all other health issues. How to overcome the guilt for prioritizing yourself? You can start by thinking like this:

- Nurturing yourself nurture and strengthens your abilities.
- You can't help anyone when you are sick.
- No one benefits if you don't feel well, but everyone benefits from a healthy, happy Empath.

You are sympathetic and sensitive, and you shouldn't view these traits as weaknesses. You also shouldn't feel compelled always to be supportive to other people and open to internalizing other people's problems. Taking in others' issues is useless, as the negative energy doesn't even disappear from the other person's life—it only multiplies. If you choose to feel others' pain and anxiety as your own, you're not helping them. You are merely doubling the amount of depression and anxiety. One of your goals is also to learn to attune to your own inner system. Along with learning how to distinguish your own emotions from the signals you are receiving from the outside.

Emotional Balance Is Your Goal!

When you are in balance, your strengths are high, and you're very driven and creative. However, when you fall out of balance and burn out, you can easily experience all the symptoms of extreme exhaustion, as well as anxiety and depression. You can spend your life going from one extreme point to another without the proper understanding of how to recover. You want to make it your daily goal to stay in balance and avoid burning yourself out.

Your imagination can be one of the biggest trends in terms of everyday life and career advancement. It can cause problems and come in the way of the accurate interpretation of the signals around you. Simply put, it can cloud your judgment. You can start to imagine situations going on when they, in fact, are not. , you can assume that you know what is happening in someone's mind instead of relying on factual evidence. You need to practice distinguishing the real signals from your imagination, and you can do this by asking yourself whether you are receiving or creating. Receiving cues and creating based on them are the two completely different feelings, and it shouldn't be hard to learn how to tell the difference.

Tuning into the imagination is dangerous because it can make you feel paranoid, pessimistic, and judgmental. If you attune yourself to the false image of what someone else might be thinking and how the situation will unravel, it can be detrimental to your health. You may become stress out or scare in advance over the circumstances and outcomes that haven't yet happened. Then suffer a load of negativity as a result of that.

You can even misunderstand what people are saying to you and give their words a more negative meaning than they truly have. You can also become overly sensitive and create illusions in your mind that can end up guiding your life and actions in the wrong direction.

Despite all of the difficulties, being an Empath is still better than being a non-sensitive person. It is a quality that you should cherish and nurture within yourself.

Feeling like You Don't Belong

You might feel like you don't fit in due to the illusion of separation. There aren't many people who understand you, and so you may decide to block out your empathy. This might lead you to view yourself as a victim of the world. You aren't drawn to drama and excitement like most people, and you're not very keen on small talk. Many Empaths feel like aliens. Understanding how you are different and connecting with those who are similar to you will help you overcome this obstacle.

You also have different perspectives from those around you.

Early Childhood & Adult Emotional Problems

You might be born sensitive, but the way you were raised can also have something to do with your sensitivities. Sensitive (empathic) children have different needs than the average, and they require more emotional education. Most parents don't nurture the self-reflection and emotional intelligence an empath needs to grow empowered. Emotional literacy is necessary for you to understand and manage your feelings. You should have been taught how to manage your emotions by your parents, and if you weren't, you might have encountered difficulties in adult life. Processing feelings and understanding your own role in creating them is crucial for a healthy emotional life. Many parents and teachers have problems with understanding their own emotions. They are unable to explain to the children how to process their own feelings.

If you were raised up in a family that practiced the wrong strategies to deal with their own emotions, it would have established problems for you. This is true even if you weren't a highly sensitive person. Parents who saw sensitive as a weakness saw the need for a sensitive child to toughen up. They actually could have also contributed to developing the wrong coping strategies like avoidance, surprising emotions, and not addressing true feelings. If your parents raised you to feel like you are wrong in some way because you're overly sensitive, you've learned many negative self-beliefs and assumptions that are now subtly guiding your life.

For this basis, it is critical to stop thinking about your empathy as a problem and start using it as a gift.

Here's What Not to do as an Empath:

- Don't try to be tougher;
- Don't think of yourself as a victim;
- Don't believe that you are not good enough if you aren't as tough as everyone else;
- Don't be overly judgmental of yourself;
- Don't be hard on yourself for frequently crying and feeling anxious;
- Don't beat yourself up for not liking confrontation; and
- Don't give in to avoidance.

This chapter aims to explain the nature of the Empath's emotional sensitivity and highlight the importance of self-love and self-acceptance in finding emotional balance.

For an empath to find the emotional balance, it is crucial to stay centered and introspective in analyzing your emotions and thoughts. For an empath, the understanding of the responsibility and accountability for one's own feelings empower self-control. By understanding that you have the responsibility for your emotional responses, as they depend solely on you, you gain the upper hand in all aspects of life.

Chapter 6: Understanding Energy

Each and everything in our Universe is composed of energy. Both organic and non-organic matter, while appear to be made from different materials are, in fact, only a collection of different energies. As a human, you think of yourself as very different from a tree. But are you, really? The matter that shapes all physical forms around us is made out of different molecules and molecules from atoms. If you remember your science lessons, atoms are nothing but pure energy in various forms. In a way, you are "one" with the entire universe because, technically, on a molecular level, all that exists in the Universe and on Earth boils down to energy. This chapter will clarify the role of energy in your experiences, as well as provide useful knowledge to keep your energy healthy and free-flowing (Orloff, 2017).

How this concerns you? As an empath, you are more sensitive to vibrations and changes in energies around you. Your neurological system enables you to detect more subtle changes than the average person. Also, these energies have a stronger impact on you than they have on a non-sensitive person. People, animals, plans, ant elements all have a subtle energy field surrounding them. These energy fields have different properties, and as an empath, you might be sensitive to them to a varying degree. Your natural sensitivities determine whether your energy field will interact more closely with those of other people, plants, animals, or natural elements.

Scientific findings suggest that the electromagnetic fields surrounding the brain and the heart also might be sending out the information about thoughts and feelings. As an empath, you are more sensitive to these signals than the average person. You can also become easily overwhelmed by this information. On top of that, your responses, both physical and emotional, to different changes in the environment are also stronger. Even events such as the changes in the magnetic field of the Sun may affect your body and the state of mind.

Besides that, your own energy field is susceptible to changes depending on your health and wellbeing. When you are filled with tensions, distress, sadness, and fear, this can intervene with a healthy flow of energy through your body and create blockages.

Why Are You Drained and Tired?

Whenever the negative influences on your energy body prevail, you will feel bad. Due to numerous reasons, you'll find yourself both tired and restless at the same time, always out of focus, drained, and unmotivated. The longer you maintain in this state, the tougher it will be for you to recover. You are naturally more sensitive to shifts in the energies around you, which can contribute to feeling drained and overwhelmed. Not to mention, being in contact with negative people and spaces can also have a detrimental impact on your energy field. For this reason, Empaths and highly sensitive are recommended to negativity as much as possible. Since removing all negativity from your environment isn't possible, you should practice energy clearing, grounding, and centering as much as possible.

How to Nurture Your Empathic Energy

Your wellbeing depends on the healthy flow of energy through your body. The daily stress causes the energy to rise to your head when it should be balanced and centered in the core of your body. There are numerous ways to work on healthy energy flow. Yoga, Qi Gong, meditation, prayer, and self-reflection are only some of them. While you can consciously, and willingly, let go of all negativity, it requires a high level of awareness that most people don't have. Most Empaths have experienced a significant amount of distress in their childhood, which caused them to harbor profoundly negative core beliefs. These beliefs are affecting your energy. So to strengthen your will and ability to heal your energy field with your mind, you first need to be genuinely able to release the negativity.

Protect Your Energy from Negative Influences

There are many ways in which you can protect your energy from harmful impacts.

Shielding is a process in which you meditate on visualizing a protective shield surrounding your body. There are many different shielding visualizations that you can use, depending on your sensitivities and the control you have over your abilities.

Grounding is another way to clear out negative energies. Grounding is a simple process that requires you to be in direct contact with the soil or another natural element, like water. You can release the negative energy both into the ground and the water, depending on which you prefer. There are countless ways to unblock your energy with grounding, from taking a walk barefoot, to taking a long shower or a bath.

Meditation is another way for you to clear out the negative influences and replenish your energy. There are numerous forms of meditation, and you can combine it with other techniques for a better effect. For example, you can meditate while grounding, which will have a profound, relaxing impact.

If you choose to arrange your space by the principles of Feng Shui, you will ensure a healthy flow of energy through your living space and your office. To further protect yourself from negative influences, you can turn to sacred objects and cleansing rituals.

Heal Others

Many Empaths can heal others by tuning into their energies. While many can heal, most choose to take energy rather than let it flow. You can't heal another; you can only enable them to do their own healing. There is a remote healing, psychic healing, healing with prayer, and healing by tapping into others energy. You can encourage someone to heal. While there's nothing that is entirely incurable. The more you know, the greater will your skills be to heal. You can't force healing, and you have to let it happen naturally.

As an empath, you can be a natural healer by sensing what the person in distress needs. You do that by tapping into their energy. If a person truly wants to heal, they will learn as much as they can about their disease and make a devoted effort to overcome it. You, as a healer, with your knowledge, may be able to pick up on what the person needs. Aside from this, you can send your prayers and healing energies to help the person heal. Keep in mind that you can't, and shouldn't, try to influence and force this process. Doing so will only drain you, and it won't be of any help to the person. The healing must happen naturally.

To truly help someone who does ask for you in desire for you to heal them, you can do so by assisting them in understanding if and why they might have, on an individual level, chosen to be sick. They may have slowed down or blocked their own healing. This doesn't mean that you should blatantly tell a person that they have chosen to make themselves sick. But that they should determine whether there is a particular aspect of the illness that they feel hard to let go. For many, being ill means a break from having to face the difficulties and challenges of life. If there's a sense of relief associated with being sick, they may be slowing down their own recovery to delay having to face their difficulties and challenges. You may sense and notice this in a person, but pay attention to share only when you feel like the person is open to understanding you correctly. Otherwise, they might feel like you are accusing them of their own disease.

Eat With Gratitude

Foods carry energy. Even if you prepare the food when in a bad mood, it may not feel right for your body. Long term, foods can have significant repercussions on health. Your negative thoughts and emotions can pass into your food and into yours and another person's body. When you feel in tune with nature, you will know what needs to be done. Focus on gratitude when cooking and eating your food.

Before you eat, bless your food. Express your appreciation for the food and express that you assure that the gift will not be in vain.

While it is all right with thanking God for the meal, also make sure to appreciate the source of the meal. Try to make your diet as organic as possible. Organic food doesn't contain the toxins and additives that are harmful to your body. Make sure to send your love and blessings to the foods that you are about to eat. You can visualize this food as being made out of energy and universal love. This way, you will wash out all the remaining negativity. If the food you are eating was made by a person who is in a bad mood, you could catch that negative energy, so make sure to cleanse it before eating.

As an empath, you can sense whether a particular food is good for you or not. Listen to your gut, literally. Refrain from eating the foods that just don't feel right.

Receive Help with Gratitude

Most Empaths find it difficult to receive support and gifts for the good that they have done. While Empaths enjoy giving, they take it as a sign of failure if something comes to them undeserved. Accepting help might make you feel like you are weak, incompetent, and undeserving. What's more, accepting compensation for your services might make you feel like your service is of lesser value. Pay attention to open yourself to receiving help and gifts because, otherwise, you are also blocking your own flow of energy. Allowing someone to help you means that they are giving gratitude. This way, you are allowing them to demonstrate their true good nature.

In this chapter, you've learned how and why the surrounding environmental energy concerns you as an empath. By nurturing the health of your own energy field, you are also taking good care of your body and mind. Furthermore, when your energy is healthy, centered, and free-flowing, you will be able to use it to benefit others. You can keep your energy clean and healthy with healthy foods, gratitude, grounding, shielding, and prayer. Still, to be a part of the positive, loving energy flow, you also need to learn to receive help and love. Giving without receiving will also block your energy, no matter how hard you try to protect it from other influences.

Chapter 7: Spiritual Sensitivity as an Empath

For an empath, nurturing your inner being is as indispensable as paying attention to your physical health. There are many effective mindful practices. You can use many of them to stay in tune with your inner being and keep your thoughts and feelings in balance. In this chapter, we will review the nature of the Empath's spiritual awareness and offer useful strategies for keeping yourself grounded and centered during all of the stages of spiritual development.

The level of empathy is a stage of awareness of your own spiritual abilities. It also refers to the level to which you've activated your skills. While most people are empathetic to a certain degree, not all of them are consciously aware of their spiritual potentials. Confidence issues may have a lot to do with how much you are willing to acknowledge your empathy because you feel like it will further isolate you. Once an empath becomes aware of their distinctive traits, their spiritual journey usually contains the three main stages, which are:

- Awareness,
- Empowerment, and
- Maturation.

Awareness

Awareness is the initial stage of the Empath's spiritual awakening. Without realizing and understanding the true nature of your sensitivity, you might feel afraid of your experiences and feel the need to block them out. At the stage of awareness, you are learning more about your sensitivities and the ways to nurture it.

Empowerment

At the stage of empowerment, you are learning how to use your skills and navigate your energy. You are aware that you have a choice in giving and receiving, and you're starting to prioritize your own health over duties to others. At this stage, you are also adopting the healthy routines of nurturing physical, mental, and spiritual health. The main challenge of this stage is to make peace with both the physical (medical and psychological) and spiritual knowledge. Modern living philosophy sort of separates the two, viewing the scientific and the spiritual as the two opposing sides. The more you learn about the spiritual, the more you'll realize that it goes hand-in-hand in science. For example, learning about the entities, which we'll explain later in this chapter, can be intimidating. Your inaccurate previous knowledge compels you to view them as threatening supernatural forces. However, if you open your mind to learn accurate information, you'll notice the similarity between this concept and how, for example, psychology views negative thoughts and rumination. The exciting part of the journey is in the fact that, while there are many blanks to fill, reading and learning will contribute to understanding the same constructs from different points of view.

Maturation/High-level empathy

As a mature empath, you have a good grasp of your gifts, and you are entirely in control over the circulation of the energy within you. High-level Empaths are very aware and in tune with their inner self, which doesn't mean that they have full control of their abilities. As a high-level empath, you can be sensitive to people whether they are around you or not.

How to Nurture Your Spiritual Sensitivity

There are numerous beneficial techniques that you can use to grow spiritually, deepen your own awareness, and sharpen your ability to interpret the experiences.

Meditation

Meditation is a practice that is scientifically proven to help overcome physical and mental overwhelm. The primary purpose of meditation is to allow yourself the time to shut the world out completely. To be in the present moment within your own body, clearing your mind and breathing deeply and evenly. It is a simple act of both physical and mental relaxation that most people benefit from, particularly if you're an empath. If you're new to meditation, guided meditations are a better option as you're receiving active guidance and instructions to relax and keep your breathing even. Daily meditation is recommended, optimally 30 minutes each day.

Journaling

Many Empaths find it beneficial to clear their minds and analyze their thoughts and emotional life. Daily journaling is helpful to unwind before bedtime and clear out any remaining negativity that might pile up during the day.

There are numerous forms of journaling. The most beneficial way to the journal is to lay out all of the situations which impacted you during the day. Include both positive and negative. Describing the situation in detail, and in particular, distinguishing the thoughts from the feelings that those thoughts have caused, is a good way for you to establish your course of mind and thinking patterns. If you're working toward establishing clear boundaries with your environment, you can lay out all of the negative thoughts to try and trace the false beliefs that they are resonating with.

For example, if you're overwhelmed with the sense of guilt, you will benefit from discovering the guilty feeling. This includes the thoughts that are resonating with these feelings. Learn which of your assumptions were inaccurate, and in particular to determine how you'll react in the same situation further on.

Moreover, journaling will help you discover the core beliefs you should change for the sake of your own wellbeing. Some of them being that you have to be generous and giving, that you owe the world to be honest, or that the world is unfair. By rationalizing your own irrational beliefs, you will empower yourself to navigate your own emotions better and observe the inner, emotional responses with more consciousness. In return, this gives you more control over the feelings you'll associate with particular thoughts. Journaling can help you not only relieve stress but to guide the process of empowerment in the long run. Reading through your journal will help you track your progress and better notice and appreciate your personal growth. This will, in return, help strengthen your confidence and self-esteem.

Praying

Religious rituals have been proven to help in recovery from all sorts of unfavorable mental and physical conditions. How you approach religion, however, should be very measured and balanced. Having a mentor or a spiritual guide, who is qualified to interpret the scripture of your religion accurately is helpful to avoid inaccurate and negative interpretations of the prayers and religious texts. Given that sacred scripture is highly symbolic and philosophical in nature, with complex metaphors given to depict the daily moral struggles, you want someone by your side that is compassionate but also at the same time rational in guiding you through the understanding of it.

Most religions have a compassionate, loving outlook on a human, but different phrasing can resonate with you in the wrong way if not understood properly. Particularly concerning man's imperfect nature. You don't want to misinterpret the scripture so that you believe that it is judging you or considering you bad in any way. Concerning other people, you want to talk to your mentor about balancing out the altruistic with your right to boundaries and your own self-esteem. Most religions recommend a patient, loving relationship, selflessness in giving, but that too shouldn't go to the extreme. A qualified religious teacher will provide you with a more in-depth explanation of these moral paradigms, helping you to understand where your boundaries should be.

Grounding

Throughout the day, your thoughts, feelings, and experiences are collecting inside your mind and body, creating the energetic blockages we call stress. Over time, these disturbances of the normal flow of energy through the body can result in physical illness. For this reason, grounding practices are beneficial to release that excess amount of energy and regain a healthy stream of energy throughout your body. There are numerous grounding techniques for you, such as connecting with nature or meditating in nature, being near water or going for a swim or practicing yoga and qigong.

Protection

The protection strategies, like shielding, and the use of sacred objects, help cultivate an open and conscious relationship with your spirituality while staying neutral to exterior influences.

The Example of Shielding

Shielding is the process in which you visualize a barrier between you and the rest of the world to stop the negative influences. It has a beneficial mental impact because, while envisioning a physical shield that protects your body, you are acknowledging your right to detach from the external influences. While doing a shielding visualization, you can picture the white light to release toxic energy. This lessens the probability of being overwhelmed with daily experiences.

Chapter 8: Spiritual risks that the Empaths should be aware of

The increased level of spiritual sensitivity makes an empath more prone to negative influences. The relationship that you have with your inner being and the energy around you has both the positive and the negative aspects.

On the bright side, your spiritual sensitivity heightens your senses and makes it easier for you to find joy and fulfillment.

Increased sensitivity to dopamine means that you need less of it to be happy. With an increased level of sensitivity to dopamine, you are easily satisfied with just staying alone with your book rather than needing a crowd of people to entertain you. You require less outside stimulation to feel pleasure, and simple things like meditation and walk around the park can make you feel fulfilled. Also, synesthesia is present in Empaths to a certain degree. With synesthesia, you are combining and experiencing different stimuli using multiple senses. For example, smelling tastes or tasting words. In Empaths, the mirror-touch synesthesia is present in the form of feeling the exterior stimuli inside themselves. These specific traits make your spiritual life more productive and happier but also more vulnerable. In the following sections, we will discuss some of the spiritual challenges that Empaths face.

Ungroundedness and Mind-Traveling

Being "ungrounded" means not being present at the moment, in your body, but instead, retreating into your own mind. This can create a sense of distance from the outside world. It can be harmful to an empath who hasn't learned to focus and bring their attention to the present moment once they choose to or when needed. Retreating to your imagination ungrounds you, especially when you are bored. High-level travels with the mind are universal with psychics, but they also come with risks. Mind-traveling is a tool that may or may not be useful to you. While you may travel with your mind, your awareness is mainly here. At any stage of empathic development, the feeling of "not being present" can occur if you don't pay enough attention to grounding and centering yourself. Furthermore, the vivid imagination and love for mind-traveling can also contribute to becoming detached from the world around you. The higher the stage of awareness, the more imperative it becomes for you to focus on staying fully present.

Mind-traveling is enjoyable for Empaths. You may daydream about nature, people, or future plans. The vivid imagination helps you focus thoughts to the ideas that are closer to your true self, rather than going through your day filled with tension. It is all right to make your mental life more meaningful and spiritually-oriented. However, staying in your mind for too long isn't beneficial because it can get in the way of being fully present. By being in your head for too long, your skills to focus on the things you are doing at the current time might weaken, and you may start to feel like you can't concentrate when you want to.

Most Empaths experience wanting to be actively present in their current activities. It could be with their friends or work, but their minds appear to be stuck inside their own thoughts. This state is the consequence of the lack of grounding. While daydreaming can be useful to stay in tune with your inner strengths, its effectiveness depends on what you are using it for. For example, if you're daydreaming about getting away from a stressful situation, it's not going to be helpful. On the other hand, daydreaming about visualizing the answers to your questions, self-reflect, and learn, is useful.

Remember, daydreaming is not a strictly empathic ability. There's nothing unearthly or supernatural about it. It is an ability familiar to all people. At any rate as a highly sensitive person, you can use it to extract the information that can help either you or another person.

Forcing daydreaming without proper education can have detrimental effects, particularly if it becomes hard to control. For example, if you've daydreamed for long periods to distance yourself from a negative situation mentally, the process can start to trigger on its own spontaneously. It might be hard for you to get back into the present moment.

Empaths often unground with daydreaming due to the lack of self-confidence. To stop this, try to stop yourself from trying to please others and to accommodate everyone. Don't apologize for who you are. You blame yourself for everything, which can lead to depression and the ungrounding as a way to mentally distance from the inner self-criticism.

Picking up on others' feelings will become easier once you establish your boundaries. For an empath, it is easy to get lost not only in your emotions but also in those you are sensing. Along with that, the fantasies that stem from internal problems and desires you may have. To recover from this state of mind, getting yourself back into the present moment is a must, with a regular routine of meditation, grounding, and centering. Staying centered will help you accept that, if someone feels bad, you don't have to absorb it. It will help you establish control over this process. Sharpen your instincts. This will tell you if someone is telling you the truth or trying to manipulate you.

Emotional Contagion

The phenomenon of emotional contagion is commonly present in Empaths. While science proves that the majority of people pick up on the emotions of those around them, this ability is intensified in Empaths. Syncing in one's system to another is an integral part of relationships and bonding with the other person. The nervous system of the empath is porous; it is less defensible than that of an average person. An empath must learn how to build up their defenses and choose the people they want to sync in with.

Food and Substance Addiction

While empathy is a beautiful gift, it can affect multiple areas of your life. In terms of health, empathy can make you feel overwhelmed, exhausted, or fatigued. Due to the overwhelming of stimuli, and particularly prolonged exposure to negative influences, you might experience fatigue, migraines, fibromyalgia, chronic pain, and allergies, as well as the adrenal fatigue.

To numb your sensations, you might turn to substance abuse and start using drugs or alcohol, as well as sex or shopping. Obesity and other dietary issues aren't unheard of either. Many Empaths use food and eating to ground themselves. What's more, the extra layers of fat might feel sheltering.

Wrong Conclusions

While you should learn how to trust your instincts, that doesn't mean that you have to draw quick conclusions. Giving people the benefit of the doubt in case you are wrong is a common sign of mature empathy. You can always choose who to accept and whether or not you want to open yourself up to them. Allowing others to take advantage of you stops them from learning and growing, as it is harming you. To prevent yourself from drawing premature conclusions, pay attention to these crucial facts:

- You can't control others' emotions or behaviors; you can just offer a different perspective of a situation.
- You are not obliged to fix other people, nor are you responsible for the consequences of their actions.
- The same way you need to stop assuming how others are feeling and thinking, you need to learn how to be emotionally independent. You

must stop expecting others to handle your problems.

Transmutation

Transmutation means changing one energy for the other. Some Empaths change their energy for others and match their energy. In terms of changing energy, Empaths can be self-destructive and try to hurt themselves to hurt others. This can happen if an empath feels judged, and they point their criticism inward instead of confronting the situation. As a result, you may be hard on yourself and even act in self-harming ways to punish those who have criticized you. The path to overcoming this pattern is to understand that you neither have the right to, nor you can control how someone else will act. The next step is to evaluate the relationships in question because those who are actually compassionate will wish to understand and acknowledge your circumstances. They won't criticize or want to make you feel like you are less worthy.

Helping Those Who Don't Want Help

The empath who tries to help another without being asked isn't doing a service to anyone. Especially those who genuinely need to ask for healing. When you wish to help someone, think about whether they've actually called for help.

Empathy can be difficult to cope with due to the intensity of the emotional experiences, and feeling like a victim of circumstances. Also, when you try to fix someone without their permission.

Harmful Entities

Entities are the disembodied spirits on the astral level. Even solid aspects are mostly space. These energies don't use a physical body and can move at the speed of thought. There are the entities that feed of negativity, and polluted empathy is vulnerable to them. As an empath, you become open to these negative influences when you ruminate in anger or fear.

You can protect yourself from entities with meditation and shielding. While the dark and negative entities exist, you shouldn't consider them to be evil. They feed on the negative energy by creating situations to create said energy. Sending dark thoughts puts you in a negative state of mind, feeding into the growing inner tension. This can happen when you ruminate on your insecurities. Recovering from the influence of entities is best done with self-care and love, clearing out the mind, and addressing difficult people and situations with compassion, rather than anger.

Sending thoughts of love and light repels this energy. Surround yourself with light and make it a part of your shield. In your thoughts, never attack the darkness back as you will feed it and strengthen it. You need to address the negative, dark thoughts by coming from a place of compassion and love.

Losing the Sense of Self

Typical signs of empathy include feeling and picking up on emotions and signals around you. It is also often psychic on different levels. You can lose your sense of identity and not know where you end, and others begin. You feel bad for people and feel obliged to feel bad about everything wrong that happens around you. You also feel compelled to intervene with other issues even when your help isn't asked for or needed. Without the knowledge of the importance of energetic cleansing and relaxation, you may store too many influences and start to feel lost within your own mind. You are also sensitive to the negative factors of others. Feeling more sensitive as time goes by can make you feel like you are losing your mind.

To protect yourself from intuitive overload, practice frequent grounding, and centering. Also, make sure to practice good self-care and treat yourself with love and grace to be able to replenish after the overload. Tune in to your inner voice as it can guide you through life.

This chapter reviewed the specificities of Empath's spiritual life. Here, you've learned that there are different stages of awareness of your potentials. Keep in mind that the matter of your current outlook isn't a hierarchy, but rather a stage of a journey that you reach with learning. Furthermore, you've learned that, while you may have a lot of spiritual potentials, there's an increased risk from getting lost in the rumination and daydreaming. Losing the ability to ground yourself and center your energy can be detrimental both physically and mentally. To avoid this, make sure to nurture a healthy spiritual life.

Chapter 9: Health Considerations for Empaths

How to remain healthy and happy as an empath? To safeguard their good health and balance, Empaths need a clean diet, a clear mind, sufficient rest, and the proper amount of spiritual care. Sensory overwhelm can lead to long-term exhaustion and fatigue.

Identifying how to take proper care of your health will prevent overload. In this chapter, we will deeply examine the most significant health issues for Empaths and provide guidance for a healthful lifestyle. The next sections will further elaborate on the most notable health considerations for Empaths.

Energetic Exhaustion

Energy disturbances that the empath detects can cause physical symptoms. After a rush of negative emotions, you might experience fatigue and headaches. Even if it's not in your best interest, you can choose to stay attached to the people who look like they are in need. This can create a mutually toxic situation that isn't helpful to any of you. Under the influence of such relationships, you may find yourself feeling exhausted continuously.

To avoid negative energetic influences and overwhelm, it is wise to surround yourself with positive people and things. Being around positive, as an overall concept, helps you turn the attention away from the intense negative feelings. On the positive side, your friend circle is most likely understanding of your traits. On the other hand, you also want to work toward empowerment, resilience, and autonomy as to not have to withdraw from negative influences, but rather balance them with the positive ones.

Empaths often have positive-oriented friends who are aiming to live a happy and satisfying life. Being intuitive also means that you are leaning toward a meaningful career, and you love to do a lot of volunteer work. You love to spend a lot of time in nature, so you lean toward fulfilling careers that give you a sense of higher purpose.

Harmful Relationships

What about your relationships as an empath? Every person needs a companion, and so do you. It is common for Empaths to be vulnerable to toxic relationships, but that doesn't mean that you are doomed to be a doormat for the rest of your life. It is not that being an empath somehow draws the toxic, abusive people into your life. You tend to look for those who need help and support that may lead you toward harmful people. Keep in mind that people like narcissists and sociopaths are people with profound problems of their own, and you're picking up on that.

What's more, some Empaths have a natural tendency to be codependent. They are looking for someone to rely on, and they easily give over the control of their life to other people. People like narcissists and sociopaths can sense when someone is easily dominated. This means you'll also have to work to empower yourself and strengthen your defenses to establish more autonomy in relationships.

At work, you might feel drained by the energy vampires. At this time, you will need developing skills and mechanisms to not only protect yourself but also have a successful working relationship with these people. If your work environment is excessively stimulating, you may need to learn how to replenish yourself to remain healthy, focused, and energized.

As an empath, your senses are sharpened, and you're more intuitive, meaning that you have increased abilities of perception. You also might develop close relationships with animals and have vivid dreams that have a strong emotional effect on you for days to come.

The upside to being an empath is the intuition and the ability to bond with others very closely. It's great to be able to read people and experience the fullness of life and nature. You are highly inspired, creative, and imaginative. You are eager to help others and in tune with your own emotions. You are very compassionate and like to look at the big picture. You appreciate and care for the world and nature around you. However, learning how to balance out the intense sensations and claim your own right to respond or not respond is a journey that will take exercise.

You are the one who has to learn how to establish your own boundaries. While having the ability to bond is genuinely pleasant, taking control over that ability is truly necessary. You need to learn how to give and receive with measure, and in a way that is not overwhelming. You can learn how to draw calmness from contact with water or unconditional love from the relationship with your pet. But, what you also need to learn is to have control over that relationship and not make it codependent. For example, loving your pet is an excellent quality.

Being able to exchange the emotion of pure, unconditional love and affection is rewarding and healing. If you accept the unhealthy attachment that your pet might feel for you, an issue that non-Empaths can experience, you can easily fall into the trap of not being able to physically separate from your pet. This is unhealthy to you both. Also, you might even start to compromise other relationships due to that relationship. For example, you might refuse to go to places where your pet can't go or socialize with people who don't appreciate animals in their home.

As you can see, the ability to establish profound connections needs to be balanced so that the relationship is more attainable and flexible. Not creating control can quickly turn into a codependent relationship. A codependent relationship of any kind is doomed to fail, taking down everyone involved with them.

Overstimulation

Allowing everyone's energy and issues into your own can genuinely harm your health on all levels. It is detrimental to you considering you genuinely do not have the duty, or you can handle everyone's problems. If you're carrying a belief that you are somehow inclined to help everyone who crosses your path, you need first to acknowledge that you aren't. Not even the greatest, wealthiest philanthropists of the world can impact the world in this way, and neither do you.

Second, you need to realize that by giving your own energy and resources to everyone, or to the wrong people, you are neglecting yourself. As well as the small number of those who can genuinely benefit from your help. The truth is, if you look into the rationale behind the altruism, you'll see that the most significant impact you can have is to be understanding to those who genuinely deserve it. We are talking about a small number of people who only need you to hear them out without judgment. If you think about it like that, acknowledging that you aren't responsible for solving everyone's problems, but you do have a choice in providing emotional support, you'll gain the ability to focus on those who are worthy of your gift and personal investment.

You might enjoy different times to unwind, and for many, the night is the time when the world becomes quiet, and you can replenish your energy. When you're alone, mediation and practicing shielding is a beneficial activity for you to get accustomed to sheltering your own body of energy. Engage in this until it becomes your new normal.

Self-Care for Empaths

Being more sensitive to the external stimuli means that you will have to put in a lot more effort into taking good care of yourself than the average person. To an empath, this might be a challenge as you're naturally more prone to take care of others than yourself. Here are the basics of the excellent self-care for Empaths:

Physical

You will need to take good care of your physical body to stay healthy, both physically and mentally. For an empath, a nutrient-dense diet becomes that more important since you're more sensitive to nutrient deficiencies. Proteins and minerals are as equally important to you as the fiber and the vitamins. You want to keep your diet as clean as possible, avoiding heavy and greasy foods. Focus on light, natural, organic foods to keep your body healthy. Minerals, in particular, Zinc, Copper, Calcium, and Magnesium, are essential to keep your body balanced. While you want to keep your mineral intake rich and constant, make sure to have a correct amount of Magnesium before bedtime and Calcium during the day to keep the levels of both in check. When recovering from a burnout, your natural compass can fall out of balance, making it harder for you to fall asleep at night and stay awake during the day. This is where balancing the Calcium and Magnesium in your diet plays a pivotal role. These minerals are helping nourish your neurons and reestablish the lost balance in your brain chemicals. Being overwhelmed is keeping you trapped in the state of constant alertness. If you've been like that for a very long time, your body will need help in finding the balance. Not only with the right foods, but also supplementation. It is required to calm your body down to the optimal levels, and then help re-teach it when it should be sleeping and when it should be awake. While fruits and vegetables are a must in every healthy diet, you also need to pay attention to taking sufficient lean protein and minerals. Meat, dairy, and a smart choice of drinking water are excellent resources for regaining the mental balance.

What Makes You Different From An Ordinary Person In Terms Of Diet?

You are more sensitive to negative dietary influences. While most healthy people can enjoy occasional cheat meals and be quite all right, you're most likely to suffer the consequences of a single unhealthy meal for days to come. This is why reducing sugar and cutting out sweets, as well as saying goodbye to the junk foods and everything fried and greasy, is essential. An ordinary person's system will suffer the consequences of an unhealthy diet only after a lot of time has passed, but not you. You will experience after a single heavy meal for days to come. This is because your body cleans up these foods slower, and your neurological system is extra responsive to detrimental nutrients such as food additives and refined sugar. You can't get away with cheat meals as quickly as most people can. A single dose of sugar might produce a healthy physical and mental response, pushing you further into the fatigue and exhaustion.

Water Choices

You want to be careful about the water that you are drinking, aiming mainly for the highly mineralized waters that are beneficial to your nervous system. You want to stay away from the bottled water as well. It is nutrient-poor and often contains toxins from the plastic packaging to which you are more sensitive than the average person.

Exercise

Your activity choices should also be different than what works for a non-empath. You might not benefit from daily jogging, outdoor sports, or working out at the gym. Your nervous system is more sensitive to the crowds and the sounds, as well as high-intensity workouts. Most Empaths find it beneficial to practice moderate daily activity in the fresh air rather than intense indoor workouts. It may be more helpful for you to practice relaxing walks in nature or low-intensity mountain hiking. With the addition of moderate-intensity activities like gardening can be found useful, not only in terms of exercise but also for mental relaxation. If you do enjoy a bit more intense physical activity that still has a relaxing impact, outdoor work and craftwork is an excellent way to give your body a boost of energy without the mental overload.

This chapter reviewed the most important health risks and considerations that an empath should be aware of. Everyday struggles for Empaths include becoming overly stimulated and burning out as a result. In this chapter, you've learned the importance of the right diet and energy replenishment to avoid overstimulation and recover from burnouts. Learning how to cope with these challenges will enable you to enjoy the advantages better and regain personal power and autonomy.

Chapter 10: Everyday Challenges Empaths Confront

How to overcome the most frequent challenges that the empath faces? Daily, you are bombarded with sensory stimulation that often feels overbearing. While most people can filter out the non-relevant signals coming from the environment, you have a difficult time. You need to control not only the messages that come your way but also your intense responses to them. There are many strategies for you to learn how to confront the negative influences without being overwhelmed by them. This chapter will review the daily challenges the Empaths face, as well as the useful strategies to overcome them.

Intense Sensations

You might be feeling a lot more stimuli from the environment, such as electromagnetic fields and radio waves, in a way that is a lot more intense than in an average person. You might be able to sense the emotional activity and thought patterns, having emotional responses to each of those considering that your physical senses have a lower response-bar.

One of your sensitivities is that you are instantly aware of the lack of harmony in the environment. Because your sensory system is so sensitive and responsive, it is easy to get overwhelmed and be unable to interpret all of the stimuli coming from the environment. You can detect that there is something wrong about the situation before there is any actual physical proof of it.

How to Prevent Sensory Overload

To prevent overload, you need first to change your mindset. The reason you have to think differently is in the fact your system responds differently than that of an average person. You can get out of balance more quickly and easily, but it takes a lot more time for you to recover.

One of the reasons why when you have a physical ailment, it won't be enough for you to visit the medical practitioner. It is your body and mind which are more sensitive to the psyche than usual. As a result, your symptoms more closely relate to the psychological and emotional. Aside from getting physical treatment when you feel bad, you instantly have to address the emotional issues that might have contributed to the disease. Address the underlying problems. Think about how the past events could have added to the symptoms that you are experiencing right now.

Headaches

While most average people will have a headache if they are overtired, you could get a headache from sensing the tension in the group of people around you. Another challenge you might face is the difficulty to determine the possible causes of your headaches. To discover the actual reasons behind the feelings of distress, ask yourself these questions:

- How much of the distress you are currently feeling is being triggered by the sensations in your body?
- How many of the painful sensations appear to be the result of environmental influences?

If the causes of your distress feel more internal than external, give yourself better self-care, more rest, and a nutrient-richer diet. However, the causes of your distress appear to be coming from the outside, practice meditation, and shielding to strengthen your will against receiving harmful influences.

Avoiding Confrontation

As you receive other people's feelings more than an average person, standing up for yourself during a confrontation might be challenging. As an Empath's natural tendency is to strive toward harmony, avoidance is frequently present. To avoid the overwhelm of negativity, you might be withholding from speaking out or letting the people around you know that you're uncomfortable. There are ways for you to navigate a conflict, using your natural gifts of compassion and the inherent listening skills, all while shielding yourself from the negative influences. Instead of staying quiet or backing up, try to do the following:

- You can confront the situation sensitively instead of aggressively. Try to remain calm and focused on the issue instead of focusing on the verbal exchange and the aggressive body language.
- By staying centered, you can successfully resolve the situation without much conflict.
- Explain given evidence on the topic, and tell people what your beliefs are.

This is far better than trying to stay silent and allowing the situation to unravel on its own.

A Lack Of Focus

Imagination probably has a significant role in your life. It can be both a positive and a negative part. While your imagination makes you more creative, innovative, and open-minded, it can also contribute to the tendency of creating unrealistic future predictions. Your imagination may cause you to have overly positive and overly negative expectations, depending on your beliefs and assumptions. Either way, finding a balanced, centered position, without the need to judge your self-worth, is the right way to evaluate the truthfulness of the creative ideas. Your sharp intuition is also helpful, as long as you've developed the ability to distinguish it from the imagination.

Trying To Control Others

You are responsible for your belief system, but you are not responsible for other adults' lives. People have the right to refuse help or choose to be angry at the moment. You have to look out for yourself first and not take on the role of resolving the conflict if the effort isn't mutual.

Instead of trying to make things right for other people, who won't make you feel better or resolve the conflict, address your own feelings. How can you make yourself feel better as you honor others?

If you try to manipulate and assume control of other people and situations, you will only get exhausted. Instead, make your own centering and balancing the focus of the situation. The resolution, in itself, is the work that will have to wait for both parties to calm down.

Stubbornness

Sensitivity, creativity, and determination can turn into a stubbornness that continually drives you to meddle into other people's problems and burn yourself out.

The Negative Self-Talk

Negative self-talk is a frequent contributor to burning out. So, how to get rid of the negative self-talk?

You will reduce the negative self-talk by unveiling the lies in your belief system or discovering the untruthful, irrational negative believes that isn't functional and accurate. This is the way for you to start rebuilding your belief system toward a more precise, balanced model.

To strengthen your defenses over constant influences, a shift of mindset is the initial step. If you don't learn how to change your mindset, you will experience a lot more stress than the average person. To survive and thrive, instead of withdrawing in the face of obstacles and anxiety, you need to learn how to change your mindset.

You need to learn how to think differently about things that are happening around you. Acknowledge that you are allowing a lot more information into the system than you can consciously process.

How to Establish Control of Your Feelings

Do you feel overwhelmed by your own feelings and unable to find a resolution for your inner struggles? One of the ways to develop the control of your feelings is to think in phrases like: "I think" and "I believe" instead of "I feel." Remember, your emotions are led by your thoughts. Try to discover what ways of thinking are navigating your emotions. Start small and expand your reflections to what is acceptable for you. An extreme would be too close yourself off. Instead, try to stay self-aware and tune into the reality of the situation. Acknowledge that you have control over your feelings and don't let the situation touch your emotions. Don't dwell on a negative situation. Acknowledge that it is not your responsibility to deal with other people's problems.

Your interpretation of the situation boils down to the inner child, who wants everything and everyone to be all right and living in harmony. You can train yourself to think differently by explaining to the inner child that it's not their job to make life right for everyone.

Learn To Be More Flexible

While you should keep your integrity and be honest with people, there is no purpose in beating the drum over issues that aren't under your control.

By learning to be more flexible, you will save your own strengths and preserve yourself better for doing the things in life that are actually meaningful, productive, and beneficial to yourself and the world around you.

Accept That Everything Is a Choice

To begin, look into why you are choosing not to have a filter, why do you want to get involved, and why are you choosing to neglect your own feelings. The negative self-talk could easily be behind these choices, as keeping yourself open, vulnerable, and passive can somewhat shift the attention away from it. The roots of this problem could easily be in your childhood.

The Balanced Empath Checklist:

- Make sure to understand and examine your own sensitivities, strengths, and weaknesses;

- Explore yourself and your emotional life with love and acceptance;
- Learn how to distinguish intuition from inner fears and desires.

This chapter reviewed the most common daily struggles of Empaths. While protecting yourself from the negative influences as much as possible is useful, it shouldn't lead to paranoia and obsession. To become more resilient and overcome the daily struggles, a balanced lifestyle, and a decent amount of self-care are a must. Aside from that, looking into the internal problems whenever a physical illness occurs is necessary to not only heal but prevent other diseases occurring as a result of neglected issues. As an empath, centering and finding the balance requires constant effort. In addition to that, becoming more emotionally resilient and skillful in a confrontation will shift your position from an energetic recipient to an influencer. Someone who can protect their own wellbeing while helping others overcome their own obstacles.

Chapter 11: Empaths, Restlessness, Exhaustion, and Fatigue

Being a highly sensitive person is associated with several symptoms such as over-sensitivity, a high responsiveness to stimuli by alertness, as well as a very high level of consciousness, creativity, and imagination. As a highly sensitive person, you process information more deeply, and you have a better ability to understand the emotions of other people.

Being highly sensitive isn't something you can change or treat. It is not a disorder. Just because you're highly sensitive that doesn't mean that there is any pathology related to you or your personality. Make sure to be aware of this because the intensity of your experiences, both physical and spiritual, might be as high as to make you question your level of rationality.

Sensory processing sensitivity entails hypersensitivity to external stimuli, greater depths of cognitive processing, and high emotional reactivity, according to scientists. But what does this mean for you? It means that you belong to 15-20 percent of the population that has increased level responsiveness to both positive and negative influences (Greiner, 2018). This makes you unique in many ways. You are also highly responsive to pain, caffeine, medicines, and other chemical influences. On the bright side, this means that you're most likely to respond to medication quickly, and you need a lesser dose of medicine to feel better. As a result of this, whether you take either medicine that your doctor prescribed you, or some homeopathic medicine, you'll feel your symptoms alleviating quickly. Much faster than the average person. On the downside, you can't afford caffeine, energy drinks, and an unhealthy diet. Taking anything that's harmful to an average body will have a faster and more harmful influence on your body.

Lower Threshold for Pain and Stress

Having increased flexibility and a higher level of responsiveness to both positive and negative influences means that you need to care well for yourself. You need to reduce the daily levels of stress to feel healthy long-term.

While being an empath can come with its own set of challenges, you shouldn't aim to subdue your gift, but instead of learning how to live and thrive with it. To

do this, you first need to learn how to care for your
nervous system.

Energetic Overwhelm

At times, you may feel overwhelmed. This is an
overload of information and energy. When you absorb
too much psychic material, you may feel
overburdened and drained. You are also sensitive to
the vibrations of things. Water is an excellent way to
cleanse your energy. Also, crystals, foods, and places
can reenergize you. It is essential to take steps to heal
your energies. If you absorb too many negative
energies.

High Sensitivity and Responsiveness

You detect the smallest changes, and others may find
you too sensitive. If you don't understand your own
qualities, you may think of yourself as weak. It is
crucial to take breaks and cleanse your energy. Never
think there is something wrong about you because
you are sensitive.

The Ability to Change Others' Energy

You can pick up on others feelings, and you can also change it. You have the potential to alter the negative by sending positive energy. If someone is in distress, you can send thoughts of healing and love. Also for yourself, is something upsets you, you can try to focus on it and declare that the issue has been healed.

Absorbing Stress and Negativity

Absorbing others' stress and negativity is another trait you'll have to learn how to control. Most people pass on their moods onto others, but if you're an empath, you'll start feeling others' stress and negativity as your own. No one really benefits from this, and you'll have to consciously develop the tools and skills to establish your own boundaries. Being increasingly sensitive to the wrongs of the world is also typical for Empaths. However, you don't have control over everything that goes on in the world. The best thing you can do is to establish which of your resources are helpful. Which are the ones you want to give without taking away anything from your own health and the quality of life? The truth is, not even if you gave up everything you have, and donated all your possessions to charity, would you make a significant difference. If you look into the history of the world, crucial changes took centuries, and it took a massive amount of engagement to progress toward altruism in society. With this understanding, you can acknowledge that you don't have to take in the cruelty and the harm of others because there are no benefits to that. You are the one getting hurt, and no one is being healed. If you have trouble coping with this, ask yourself this question: Does feeling this way truly benefits anyone? Or Does choosing to hurt in this situation truly helps anyone? The answer is, "No." Still, there's no need for you to unnecessarily expose yourself to the disturbing contents of the media either. There's nothing beneficial in watching horror movies, so you should feel free to shelter yourself from these influences whenever possible.

Burnouts and Emotional Hangovers

Emotional overwhelm can quickly leave you drained, tired, and fatigued. While you should shelter yourself from unnecessary stress, your intention, in the long run, should be to strengthen and become resilient, empowered. Not many people can block out stress or change the outside circumstances. Developing the skill of a healthy relationship with anxiety should be your long-term goal.

Your heightened intuition and instincts are your greatest assets, meaning that you can move through life with great success if you learn how to express, interpret, and trust your intuition. Opening up about your sensitivity might also be challenging because as a woman, it's very likely you've been told that you are too sensitive. Maybe you were called "mentally unstable," or even crazy, for your rich and vivid emotional life. You can find the right environment that won't be judgmental of you. However, the true, inner, self-acceptance of your qualities is necessary to prevent negative self-image, negative self-talk, and damage to your self-esteem. Ultimately, your goal is to establish balance and boundaries when it comes to dedicating your own time and effort to other people.

While thinking that you should toughen up isn't the best way for you to go about your empathy, gradually, slowly and patiently exercising to become more resilient is.

Most Empaths need to learn how to handle sensory overload that happens due to responding to the more enormous amount of stimuli than the average human body. To clarify, you are not receiving the stimuli that are nonexistent to other people. Everyone who is in the same environment is influenced by the same conditions, but it is the level of responsiveness that makes a difference. The ones who are not sensitive are merely responding to a lesser amount of stimuli. It takes a higher intensity of stimuli for them to create a neurological response than it does for you. Learning how to navigate that sensitivity will help you move on from overwhelm to empowerment.

As a result of feeling drained by overwhelming environmental stimuli, you can end up feeling lonely and isolated. And humans aren't made to be alone and isolated. While staying within your comfort zone enough to replenish is a good idea, it isn't an ultimate solution. Let's say that you are in a situation where being in society disturbs you, and being isolated makes you feel lonely and detached. What do you do? You should practice exposure gradually by slowly increasing the portions of time you will spend with people to the amount that you can handle. While it's possible that as an empath you'll always be a bit of a lone wolf, you don't have to be a lonely wolf. Remember, even wolves have packs, and you too can balance your need for solitude with the need to socialize.

Avoidance

On all levels of human health, avoidance is a coping mechanism one can confidently call unhealthy. The only way for you to overcome any obstacle is with careful, gradual exposure. Knowing what you know about empathy, you should be aware that facing the challenges should be done with a generous dose of self-love. Do this slowly, so your system has the time to adjust.

Neglecting your own needs can lead to exhaustion, depression, anxiety, and overall feeling sick. You can, however, take charge over your sensitivities and learn how to navigate the stressors that are making you feel overwhelmed. By identifying your triggers, you'll learn how to heal and prevent any damage from happening in the future. You want to approach your life without rush, and avoid staying in crowded areas for too long. You additionally want to take good care of your diet, since junk food and too much sugar only worsen the existing symptoms of sensory overwhelm.

How to Calm Your Nervous System after Burning Out

Learning how to calm down, or calm your nervous system, is one of the initial steps to learning how to strengthen your resilience to environmental stimuli and empower yourself.

To overcome the overwhelm, you should start with calming your nervous system and proceed with getting it used to function in a balanced way. This is best done with a clean, balanced lifestyle and diet, as well as with herbal medicine and supplementation. The reason why herbal medicine is so beneficial for Empaths is that floral teas and other remedies are safe to use long-term. Your sensory neurons respond to them in a way that brings relief quickly.

Recovering from burnout is part of the healing process that is more physical than spiritual. You are trying to discover where you are in the stress response pattern. The first stage of stress is called "the alarm stage." You might be in a lot of pain or suffering a lot of anxiety and fears. Your adrenaline is now heightened, and your nervous system is unable to calm down. The second stage of stress is the resistance stage. This is where you are locked into the negative cycle of stress and anxiety. This has numerous adverse effects on your body. This can happen when you've been under the influence of stress for a very long time, and you are moving toward the exhaustion stage.

These different stages require different interventions for your nervous system to calm down.

To diagnose your current health state, you can get your mineral never levels analyzed. You will need the support of the sedative minerals to reduce your stress. If you are exhausted, you will need a combination of sedative and stimulating minerals and nutrients to adjust your sleep with the activity levels. To soothe your nervous system, you can also reduce the influence of the negative people in your life.

Reducing caffeine, increasing protein, increasing magnesium, and hydration will help to calm your nervous system and alleviate the symptoms of anxiety.

Spend more time walking on the ground by yourself. Perform this while in contact with the earth, as well as doing water yoga, meditation, visualizations, and light exercise is suitable for calming your nervous system. This will serve you to become more attuned with the shifts in your energy during the day and to wind down more comfortably at night.

After you've experienced overload, you'll need to withdraw and give yourself time to recover. You will do this by staying in a quiet place, getting extra rest, and enjoying light, calming activities. Depending on the intensity of the overwhelm, you might want to retreat to a dark room and give yourself time to heal. Sleep and medication are also helpful to regain a sense of inner peace and focus.

Chapter 12: Succeeding as an Empath

Many Empaths face obstacles on their way to success due to their increased sensitivities. In this chapter, you will learn how to view yourself differently and break the myths about Empaths that might be holding you down. Furthermore, you will learn how to trigger the empowered state of mind and the importance of shifting your mindset for success.

In Empaths, the heightened sensitivity and intense experiences can lead to overwhelm. Overwhelm, and exhaustion often block the Empath's efforts to succeed in all aspects of life. Instead of blocking or suppressing, which cause additional fatigue, bringing yourself into the center (centering your energy) and finding the inner balance is your ultimate goal (Greiner, 2018). Rather than allowing yourself to go the extremes in giving in and burning out, have the balancing and centering in your mind every step you take. The next sections will discuss the common myths about Empaths.

Myths about Empaths

Due to the wrong understanding of empathy and the lack of awareness on the magnitude of Empaths' abilities, many misconceptions are surrounding those who are highly sensitive. These myths might resonate with your fears and insecurities, causing you to feel passive and powerless. Following are the most common misconceptions about Empaths.

Empaths Absorb Other People's Emotions in Energy

You have a choice in whether or not you receive other people's signals. While you have the potential to do it, you also have the ability not to do it if you choose so. You're not condemned to feel everyone's feelings because you have a choice in allowing or disallowing it.

Empaths Are Introverted

Not all Empaths are introverted. They are merely more likely to be withdrawn. Seclusion and withdrawal are the tools most Empaths use to prevent the overwhelm of stimuli. You might become an introvert as a coping mechanism. It is a learned behavior of isolation to protect yourself.

Empaths Are Magnets for Sociopaths

There's nothing in your personality that makes your target to narcissistic and sociopaths. You are not destined to be the victim of these people. You are not energetically drawing in negative and harmful people. This can happen because you are more vulnerable to their influence and prone to feeling responsible for healing those who can't or don't want to be treated.

Your task is to heal yourself from the negative influence and free yourself from giving away control of your life to other people. There is a difference in being sensitive and being fragile. You might be shying away from social situations because you are sensitive, but that doesn't make you weak. Running away could be a coping mechanism, but it is the behavior that you should aim to change. You can be both sensitive and extremely strong.

Shifting Your Mindset to Find Success

A simple shift in the mindset, where you move from feeling like a victim to acknowledging and owning your own freedom of choice, is the initial step to finding success as an empath. There are two overall stages of empathic development. On the one side, there is the disempowered state. A state in which you are under the constant influence of others and the environment. At the other end of the spectrum, there is the empowered state, in which you have established the mental autonomy, and you're in complete control over your abilities.

In the disempowered state of mind, you are using yourself as a resource to give away to gain acceptance and support. This is harmful on all levels. You are not only shying away from people and life, but you are also allowing other people to take away your power. Your resources to feel accepted. Your task here is to acknowledge your own right to say no and establish your own boundaries. In this stage, you need to realize and recognize your own right to your own limits. You also need to learn and accept that giving is a choice, not an obligation.

Core beliefs make a difference in whether you believe that the energy, or a person or situation that has presented itself, is stronger than you. If you believe that the situation is stronger than you, you will give yourself in. If you believe that you are stronger than the situation, you will become empowered. Empowered people believe that the circumstances can't overwhelm and overpower them.

Your life could completely change if you just start believing that you are stronger than the situation. Empowered Empaths believe and know that everything is a choice. Your nervous system might be porous, but you do have a choice in what you decide to allow inside your system. You can choose to not interact with a specific energy. You can choose not to take in the negative influences, but feed of the positive ones instead. The main difference is in understanding that you are the influencer of the energy instead of being influenced by it. You also have the power to become the influencer of the other energy fields.

The Shift from Powerless To Powerful

What if you feel like you can't manage your sensitivities? An Empath's natural neurological defenses are weaker than those of an average person. The intensity of the energies you take in can feel unbearable, and you may feel like you can't control it. Luckily, this can't be further from the truth.

The Shift from the Victim to the Influencer

One of the ways for you to assume an empowering position instead of deeming yourself powerless is to not think of yourself as a victim. A right way for you to frame your process of strengthening is not to expect the world to change to accommodate your needs. Why is this important? Whether the sounds around you feel too intense, or the mere presence of people fills you with the inner tension, going on the assumption that the sounds and people need to go away for you to feel better isn't the ultimate solution. Start by framing your mind to think that it is you who needs to grow resilience. Not forceful, of course, but rather gradual, steady, and self-loving all the way through. Whenever you feel like the world is too intense for you, shift your thoughts to think about the need to establish the choice and control over what you take in.

The shift from passive to accountable

Your feelings are entirely within your control, regardless of how it may seem. While you should love and accept your sensitivities, you should also take responsibility for your feelings and thoughts. This mere shift in consciousness from thinking that thoughts and feelings simply occur, to understanding that they're within your control, can completely transform how you view your sensitivities. Not to say that this happens overnight, of course. Learning to navigate the inner mechanisms that cause you to make the unconscious choices might take a lot of time, but the effort will inevitably be fruitful. Understanding your sensitivity, but also learning how to address them in a balanced way can be achieved through meditation, journaling, and self-reflection.

Here's an example of how you can move through your thought process to decrease anxiety around people:

Example:

You can't help but feel nervous around a specific person. Here are the questions to ask yourself:

- Why am I choosing to take in their energy? Do I feel obliged to do so, or I perhaps feel like I am rejecting the person as a whole if I don't take in their negative feelings?
- Why are their feelings, my responsibility?
- Is this person benefiting from me feeling this way?

- How can I filter out this influence? (Deciding that taking in the negativity is useless, mediating, shielding)

How to Become Empowered

To become empowered, you need continuous work to love and accept yourself. You need to look into your natural gifts and start to view them as tools for success, rather than sensitivities that are holding you down. What makes you different from other people as an empath is that your nervous system is more easily excitable. This means that to empower yourself and protect your energy, you will need to learn how to control the level of excitement you will allow.

Confront With Compassion

Empathy is an emotion common to most people, but to you, it has a more significant meaning. It is a state of existence. These terms, empowering means learning how to navigate your state of mind to replace judgment with understanding and compassion. This is the single way for you to be well, because, as you've learned in the previous chapters, getting angry and annoyed at people only drains you.

Create Powerful Connections

Being an empath means that you don't only understand other people's emotions, but you're able to feel them. You can leverage that to have a real, profound understanding about how the people around you feel, rather than just stop when emotion is detected. This means that you can shape your relationships to be more open and honest, and become a person whose friends, coworkers, and romantic partners will trust and open up to. Both in terms of business and personal life, you can leverage your gift to build strong, trusting connections.

Look at the big picture

You're detecting, reading, and interpreting the events around you. You can process, discover, and read the information that most people around you are unable to. You can also do this at a distant, spiritual, and physical level. You are more sensitive to the energetic level of existence, instead of only sensing physical stimuli. While you might have thought that this brings no more than overwhelming and exhaustion, it also means that you can always look at the bigger picture. Understand the background of the events and situations.

As an empath, you don't have a sensory filter that an average person has. Your energy system is more porous than that of an average person and takes less time to communicate with the outside environment. This doesn't mean that you can't train your body and mind to focus on the things you want to receive, versus those that you don't want. Your body and the nervous system are a little bit different, as your system picks up the changes in the environment more easily. While this might sound distressing, it also means that you can focus and notice what you find is important easier than other people. At work, this means that you can sense the dynamic of the organization and notice when big, significant changes are about to happen.

Self-love will help you overcome the disempowered state of mind, and nurture the empowering beliefs that help you to establish control of your emotions.

This chapter reviewed the most common myths about Empaths and explained the right ways for an empath to regain control and power over their sensitivities. In this chapter, you've learned that your sensitivities can become tools for success if you simply look at them the right way. The more you know yourself, the more you will be aware of your qualities and abilities, as well as your strengths. The moment you understand who you are, meaning that you reach the stage of autonomy, you will become empowered. The moment you start to view your authentic traits as gifts are the moment when you will realize that you can use them in a way that is beneficial to both you and everyone else.

Chapter 13: You and Your Significant Other

As an empath, you'll face many challenges with relationships. Some of the biggest struggles are to learn how to express your needs and communicate in a relationship. While a loving relationship will empower an empath, a toxic one might have substantial repercussions to your health. You deserve to be loved and cherished. This chapter will look into the most common struggles the Empaths have in romantic relationships, as well as present you with the ways to overcome them.

The Need for Solitude

Perhaps one of the most powerful features in an empath is that you are looking for a soul mate. Despite that, many Empaths are either single for prolonged periods or are stuck in toxic relationships.

While you may desire a profound relationship, a constant need for solitude and the difficulty in expressing your needs might be in the way of a quality relationship. Also, being around someone for too long might affect you in a way to become overstimulated. You might become irritated by the person even if they aren't doing anything wrong. While you have numerous qualities as an empath, you are not always easy to live with due to the sensitivity. However, that doesn't mean that you are destined to remain alone for the rest of your life.

While you are powerfully compassionate and intuitive, the overwhelm can often cause you to have intense reactions that might be hard for your partner to understand. The feeling of overwhelm can grow with the relationship, and merging with the partner's feelings don't always have the best impact on your relationship. The underlying issue might be that you, while striving toward a profound, meaningful, intimate relationship, also require solitude and independence.

Over-Attachment

One thing you should look at doing is to learn how to separate connection and attachment. As an Empath, you may seek to produce out the best in a person, believing that the person simply needs love and support to prosper. However, if this intention isn't mutual, it can quickly turn into a codependent, toxic relationship where there's an unhealthy attachment. In this relationship, you are giving but receiving nothing back. So, ask yourself whether or not the link connecting you and your partner is about the attachment. Maybe it is about the connection.

Fear of Commitment

While you may be aiming toward a relationship, you still may experience commitment issues. You might have trouble meeting a partner who will recognize your desire for solitude. Or that you carry the painful burden from previous relationships that have left you feeling hurt and disappointed. What you need to realize is that a successful relationship requires equal commitment from both parties involved.

You deserve to have your needs heard and acknowledged. You need a partner who is a good listener and very understanding of your unique traits. They should also be able to understand your intense emotions and the need to establish boundaries to protect yourself.

If you are a relationship empath, you might be absorbing the partner's emotions. You feel anxious when spending too much time together. Feeling like it takes away from your independence and identity.

Even if you love your partner profoundly, you still might prefer sleeping alone to recharge yourself.

Another thing that could make your life as an empath more difficult is being annoyed at the little sounds that the partner is making and feeling extremely exhausted after arguments.

How to Find the Emotional Compatibility

Finding a partner who attracts you isn't much of a challenge, nor encountering the people you agree with on an intellectual level. The trouble is discovering a partner with whom you're emotionally compatible as well. Emotional compatibility is all about being attuned in terms of delicate sensitivities and emotional responses. Do you align in the things that make you happy or sad? Are you compatible in terms of tolerance in the long run? Do you share an equal desire for solitude?

For this reason, looking for someone who spends a lot of time away from home due to work might not be a bad idea. On some level, you will instantly feel a spiritual connection between you and the person. However, that connection may not always be the best choice for you. While you might feel the energy connection, look into the quality of that connection. Is that connection taking away the energy from you, or is it feeding you both with positive energy? Likewise, pay attention to whether or not the individual's actions, reactions, and words match the energy you are perceiving. If you feel the desire to separate yourself from the person from the get-go, that might be a signal that this person isn't authentic.

There might be numerous types of partners who are an excellent match for Empaths.

- The quiet, intellectual type. This type of partner refers to stay at home and be inside their own mind. They are calm and rational. While this kind of person could have a positive, grounding effect on you, pay attention if they are sufficiently emotionally open and available. Pay attention to whether or not you match on a physical level in terms of the need for physical and emotional bonding. An intellectual will love to help you solve problems, but one at a time, since they don't like feeling overwhelmed. To help your intelligent partner understand you, help them know that you are communicating from the heart rather than the mind.
- Another empath. Having a relationship with a fellow empath can be fulfilling, but experiencing overwhelm simultaneously can be highly intense. Your focus should be on respecting each other's needs and staying grounded. Finding the happy middle between spending enough time apart and together is

also advisable, particularly on a daily level when both of you need enough time to unwind and relax. Be open about each other's emotional triggers, and be respectful to the boundaries, so you don't trigger each other. On the bright side, practicing meditation, grounding, and visualization together can be profoundly intimate and enforcing your connection.

- The tough, strong, silent type. As an empath, you might find great value in a partner who is strong and dependable. This type of partner won't get upset quickly. A rock-hard partner might help you learn how to balance out your emotions. To keep the relationship harmonious, frequently express gratitude to your partner because they might not be able to pick it up from your affections. Be open when asking from intimacy because this type of person isn't very good at picking up subtle cues. Both of you may find it enjoyable to spend time in nature. One thing you should help your partner with is expressing emotions.

Your tendency to make yourself open may not be of the same intensity as theirs. Make sure not to push your partner to open up. Encourage them to seek you out when they need support. It is possible for this type of person to feel like expressing emotions is a sign of weakness. Encourage them to do so not by making yourself always available but assuring them that you'd never consider them to be weak.

State Your Relationship Requirements

Being transparent with your partner in terms of needs for a relationship is a common-sense suggestion that you should follow. Overcoming the desire to please and be agreeable, as well as the dread of confronting your partner about the behaviors and situations you're uncomfortable with, is a typical struggle for Empaths. The reluctance to verbalize your needs and requirements makes it impossible for the other person to show you the love and care that you deserve. The following sections will break down the most important aspects of relationships that you, as an empath, should learn to discuss with your partner.

Communicate Your Needs

As an empath, you may have trouble communicating your own needs while simultaneously being extremely receptive and understanding to the needs of your partner. To somewhat complicate the matter, your natural inclination to creativity and imagination may compel you to create unreliable assumptions about your partner's thoughts and feelings. To a certain degree, most couples learn how to predict the ways their significant others will feel and respond. However, there's no guarantee that these assumptions are accurate. One of the strategies that you can use to assure excellent communication with your partner is always to ask if you're correct to think or assume that they are feeling, or thinking a certain way.

Ask For Personal Space

Another specificity about having a relationship as an empath is the heightened need for private space and alone time. You will most likely need a certain amount of space, or even a separate bed to be able to relax fully. The mere presence of the other person might be continually giving you different signals that might prevent you from relaxing and unwinding completely. You can go about this in many different ways. Ideally, your partner will be understanding of your needs and won't have a problem with giving you the extra space. If you or your partner feel like your need for space might be compromising the intimacy of the relationship, there are also options you can look into.

Be Clear About Your Point Of View

As with all other relationship, you need to stay open and communicate your thoughts and feelings to your partner. As an empath, you're likely to have excellent listening skills, but expressing your needs might take some work.

Male and Female Empaths

Your sensitivities and the struggles you are facing might be different depending on your gender. If you're a male empath, it is common to feel ashamed of your sensitivity and refrain even more from expressing your feelings.

The gender stereotypes present in our society might make it even more difficult for you to express your feelings. This is because you've been taught that crying is a sign of weakness. Me personally, my father always said that crying didn't solve anything. To be a strong man, you're not supposed to cry. These stereotypes make it harder for all men to establish a quality relationship, let alone a highly sensitive person. Another way being a male empath can be challenging is that you most likely don't share the interests of other males. You might not be into aggressive sports, and you're most likely not a big fan of soccer and football. As such, you may be standing out from the crowd, and you might have been teased and bullied for your distinctive traits. As a result, you might be suffering in silence and pushing down your emotions to avoid judgment.

This might have a negative impact on your health, relationships, and career. Still, strong male Empaths are numerous. If you're a male empath, embrace your qualities. Exercise to establish more control over the sensitivity will help you move from a passive, receptive position to the position of authority and empowerment.

Once you learn to establish the balance of your emotions, your strength and high IQ will shine in their best light. Your compassion will become an appealing quality that will make you irresistible. Losing the fear of your emotions and of others, as well as giving yourself the permission to express your keen intuition, can be a ticket to a successful business and useful tools for you to find a truly compatible partner.

For female Empaths, recognizing one's own emotions isn't as dangerous of an issue. The issue is to learn how to step out of the passive role and determine the real power and control of yourself and your own life. Female Empaths are more susceptible to being pleasers and putting everybody's needs before their own. As a result, a female empath is giving without reserve and failing to take care of herself in the right way. Their health issues result from being stuck in toxic relationships and giving up the power to others. Exercise your right to say no. Choose when and to whom you want to give, as well as learning to treat yourself with the ideal amount of love, care, and acceptance, is the right way for female Empaths who are.

Chapter 14: Shielding Yourself from Energy Vampires

Energy vampires are attracted to Empaths. Having relationships with energy vampires can be draining for an empath, as they feed off the Empaths energy. This chapter will present you with the various types of people who can have a toxic impact. Learn to give advice to protect yourself from their influence and build a mutually respectful relationship.

"Energy vampires" can be at work, at home or in any area of your life. They will cause you to feel ashamed and as if there's something amiss with you. You need to spot them and establish strategies to handle these types of individuals. This will stop them from influencing you. To get back your power, you need to learn how not to accept their words personally. When you meet an energy vampire, you will feel sick, fatigued, and depleted. You'll doubt yourself and become self-critical. You also might feel irritable and distressed. Occasionally, you might draw in a toxic person for sharing the same emotional issues. This can produce an unhealthy connection. If you experience low self-esteem, you can attract those who want to criticize to feel empowered.

How to Cope With Energy Vampires

Whether it is your family member or a friend, being around negative people might be detrimentally affecting health. To protect yourself from the energy vampires, you will need to establish control over the relationship, your inner response, and the mindset surrounding these toxic people. Rather than avoiding them, your goal should be to find a harmonious balance when interacting with negative people.

Here's how to start changing your mindset about negative people:

- Don't focus on the negative aspects;
- Don't compare yourself with others; and
- Don't criticize.

The words and labels you are using can have an important role in learning how to communicate with people properly. Instead of avoidance, you want to learn how to communicate clearly and concisely that signals your true feelings for the person.

Here are some guidelines for successful communication with challenging people:

- Be careful to use the right words;
- Try to shift focus from the negative to the positive ideas;
- Set your mind to finding balance with the person; and
- Try not to view people as toxic.

Believing and telling yourself that a person is toxic will create even more negativity and anxiety surrounding these people and situations. Avoid thinking that these people are attacking you and that you need to shelter yourself in some way. What you want to do is to slowly exercise and develop your own emotional and cognitive resilience to the influences of other people. You want to enforce yourself not to be easily influenced by toxic people, but rather be able to take control of the interaction and steer it into a more positive direction.

There are numerous types of energy vampires. Their toxic impact on your wellbeing depends on the kind of energy that they are attracted to.

Narcissists

Narcissists are among the most harmful people for Empaths. They act as if the world revolves around them. They use their intuition for personal gain and are prone to belittling people to boost themselves. They are deficient in empathy and unable to care about how others feel. They use emotional expressions only when there is a perceived personal gain for them.

Empaths are attracted by the charisma and the appearance of giving, thoughtful people. In the long run, these relationships are one-sided and toxic. As an empath, you lack the usual defenses and are hard to convince that some people can't be won over with love. It is hard to leave the relationship with a narcissist because they are skillful and manipulative. They can make you physically ill and harm your self-esteem. They will question your sanity and set up the situations to make you look incompetent and unreasonable.

To deal with them, lower your expectations, and don't expect them to understand and respect your sensitivity. If you can't get away from this type of a person, distance yourself emotionally from them, and don't give them ammunition to blame you for anything. Another way is to picture cutting the cord and break the bonds to free yourself from the energetic ties. Give the relationship an honorable closure. You can do this by breaking a stick while thinking that the relationship is over.

Anger

Angry energy vampires use anger to make a point, which is detrimental to your porous nervous system. They will hit below the belt, aiming at your weaknesses to beat you down. You may try to communicate the situation, but you need to be fierce about protecting your own energy versus being socially acceptable. To set limits with this type of person, understand the difference between venting and dumping. The first isn't harmful to you, and the latter affects you. If you want to preserve a relationship with this type of person, they can warn you in advance that they feel like venting. With venting, keep the same topic without placing the blame and avoiding holding yourself accountable. Another way is to let the person know that you hear them, but you can do that only when they calm down. You can set a rule not to yell. Avoid acting on impulse and make a pause whenever you feel agitated. Be careful about your speech and don't allow yourself to dump the anger, as it will drain you and make you feel depressed.

Attention

This type of person always sees themselves as a victim, and you can fall into the trap of dealing with them only for them to dismiss all of your suggestions of solutions. Don't let yourself turn into their therapist. Limit your listening time and suggest them to find a therapist. Keep a smile but still, state you disapproval loud and clear. Be polite about refusing to set the time aside for them. Break the eye contact during a conversation, and clearly show that you are not interested in their drama.

Drama

Some people feed off of drama. They get energized by others' response to the drama, so be sure to stay calm as to not feed into their drama. Never ask them how they are doing because they will always have a drama ready to insert you in. Smiling and laughing keeps the victim energy vampires away.

Criticism

These people energize of criticizing other people, and as someone who takes everything to heart, you might quickly get depressed over the constant nit-picking. You can politely ask them to stop criticizing in a non-emotional way. Find the self-esteem issue that they are triggering and heel it.

Dominance

This type of vampire disturbs with constant talking and intruding on your personal space. You shouldn't tolerate this type of person. You need to overcome your tendency to please them and set boundaries. Interrupt the person and be patient in letting them know that you are not interested in the conversation. Make a request to be heard clearly and loudly since these people don't get the verbal cues.

Passive-Aggressiveness

These people sugarcoat their aggression and are very undependable. Often goes hand in hand with narcissism. They keep forgetting to do the things that matter to you intending to annoy you. Being nosey when you need quiet time. They are sarcastic and offensive and sugarcoat this as a joke. They are not direct, and to protect yourself, don't question your opinion about them. Learn their patterns and call them out on their behavior in a leveled, calm way. Ask them to clarify their position on issues and being specific to understand them and take your power back.

With these strategies, you'll protect yourself from being harmed by the energy vampires. Setting limits will protect your sensitivity. You should also consider ending the relationships that are not working out.

While you can't change a person, you don't necessarily have to avoid them or cut them out of your life. The better idea would be to learn how to navigate the relationship so that the negative influence doesn't harm you. If you don't stop labeling people as toxic or negative, it will be difficult for you to find positive ways to navigate to the relationship. It will give you a lot of negative feelings and grief. Understand that these people have their own problems that they are unable to solve. Also, make sure to acknowledge that solving these problems is not your business either.

Learning how to cope with energy vampires is an excellent opportunity for you to grow your own emotional and communication skills, and become a stronger, more resilient empath. Focus on finding more sensitive and correct wording when talking with unbalanced people, and for how you speak to yourself, to be overall more compassionate. Think of these people as unbalanced and in need of finding a balance. There's also a possibility you could also need balancing. Make sure to concentrate on the positives of the situation rather than the negatives.

Finding balanced ways to cope with an energy vampire is always better than going to the extreme. One extreme is to do nothing and to allow the person to affect you. The other extreme is to cut yourself from the relationship. Both of these other extremes and aren't helping you or the person in question. It could be that a person who has a draining impact on you is a life-long friend. Perhaps a loving family member or a coworker with whom you simply have to find a way to get along.

So, how can you get past the negativity?

Look Within

Ask yourself: Why is this person affecting me so much? What are the beliefs and insecurities appealing to your inner self and are triggering the emotional response within you?

Offer Compassion

While you don't have to be involved with the negative person, you also don't have to think negatively about them. Adding the negativity on top of the negativity will, logically, only produce more negativity.

Don't Try To Change Them

While you can feel bad about the person, you shouldn't feel inclined to feel as bad as them. You can decide to mend the relationship, but it is entirely within your right to move on with your life. You don't need to try to fix someone who doesn't want to be fixed.

Respectfully Disengage

If you feel like someone is being verbally aggressive with you, you can say to that person that you are not ready to have a discussion. They are currently not open to hearing you out. Don't get involved with the person who is presently unable to acknowledge your opinions or move on from their negativity. Make sure to internally disengage from the emotional state of that person while acknowledging their feelings. To practice emotional disengagement from difficult people, change your mindset to establish boundaries. You will do this in the following ways:

- Don't try to help or share your opinions unless somebody asks for them.
- Don't feel inclined to take in the situation or consider it to be your responsibility to resolve the situation.
- View others' opinions as to their perceptions of the situation, not the actual truth of the situation.

Discover the Negative Triggers

There's a reason why particular conversations are triggering to you. When certain words or situations fall hard on you and trigger anger, anxiety, or fear, they are appealing to the inner criticism and self-esteem problems that you're holding within.

What you need to do is to discover what this triggering situation indeed activates inside you. What thoughts, feelings, and situations are you associating with the trigger? What could be the untruthful, irrational belief that is lying at the bottom of your outlook to the situation?

Understand that the negative people are using the said mindset to secure themselves in case something goes wrong. It is the fear, anger, and the pain derived from the profound insecurity that is driving their behavior.

Shielding Visualization

Here's how to use shielding visualizations to block the impact of an energy vampire:

- You need to sit down comfortably and start meditating.
- Focus on your breath, making your breathing deep, and even. While meditating, allow all of your thoughts to drift away and center your energy.

- When you become fully relaxed, visualize a shield extending somewhat beyond your body. You can give your shield any color you want, making sure you are sufficiently feeling your own presence within your body.
- In a fully relaxed state, express gratitude for the shield and come back to the present moment.

Chapter 15: Empaths and Employment

As an Empath, you need a serene, relaxed place of work to thrive and do your best. Your defenses against stress are weaker. You are a free-spirited person who thinks out-of-the-box, and you don't function effectively within the conventional office environments. The position that satisfies your temperament will encourage you to grow. A wrong job can suck the life out of you and damage your health in the long run.

The Perfect Work Environment

The sense of understanding, the people, the energy, and the energy of the working area has a tremendous impact on your work productivity and satisfaction. Empaths enjoy meaningful work that syncs with your sensitivities. You will enjoy doing whatever gives you a sense of meaning. You enjoy being of service and using your creativity. You can do this at any job, as wherever you work, there is someone who you are helping to. Being brave to follow your heart and intuition isn't easy, but can help you level up and grow both skills and finances. It is sometimes hard if the work that you want to do differ from what you think works best for your career.

The energy of the people you are working with affects you and having to work with the wrong people might call for additional adjustments to make the workplace work for you. You work better in people-sensitive, supporting settings, where you will find support and appreciation. Finding the colleagues you can relate to is much realistic if you can't change your job. There will be energy vampires you will have to learn how to cope with. These people can be in any workplace. Working among toxic people can be profoundly harming to Empaths as you absorb their negativity. There are many strategies to cope with these people, such as setting boundaries, shielding, and mediation. Focusing more on positive coworkers is also a good idea.

The energy of the physical space also affects you. If the workspace doesn't feel right, you won't feel all right in it. You can try to make the space more comfortable for yourself or do energy cleansing rituals. Try changing the placement of furniture and other things that make space feel more personal. Physical crowdedness, lack of light, and lack of personal space can be agitating to an empath. You can try to center the area or to center your energy within the space. To an empath, being exposed to machines and electronics is energetically and mentally draining. You can limit the use of the electronics and limit the contact with the negative people.

Emotional Contagion at Work

Emotional contagion means absorbing the stress from the environment, as well as panic. Nowadays, business spaces share the same areas, and so you can't isolate yourself from the stimuli. There are numerous ways for you to shelter yourself. This can happen at a distance as well, like over the phone. You can become anxious about work even when you are not at work.

Need for Stimulation

You are a free-spirit who bores easily and leaves their job if it isn't inspiring and stimulating enough. You need your work to be meaningful. The job that you do needs to not only inspire you but also to make you feel like you are contributing to the improvement of the world. Creativity, inspiration, and searching for the higher meaning shape your entire career.

You need to find the right work. The best jobs for Empaths are those low stress with small companies and on their own, away from the office frequency. Working from home is also popular among the Empaths. Packed schedules don't work for Empaths, as the risk of burning out is too high. You are most efficient when managing your own time, so focus on the jobs that give you the most significant possible amount of freedom.

Cohesive, positive teams feel good for Empaths, which means that you might work well within carefully chosen teams.

You don't function well in offices and prefer to be your own boss. Smells, sounds, and strong lights might not feel good for you. You might be able to negotiate part-time work from home or do it somewhere outside the office. Independence in business often helps. For example, you can work by Skype. Isolation isn't good for Empaths to, and you need a balance of being alone and being alongside people. While you enjoy working alone, you don't need to completely get away from people to be fulfilled with your work. Time management is also essential, as well as setting aside enough time for you to recover after a long day. Also, planning breaks to walk or meditate can help clear the mind midday.

You need the ability to manage your schedule and prevent overload. Most Empaths often go into helping professions but are very sensitive to being overloaded. This is the reason why the balance is crucial. The same with working to empower yourself and establish power over your ability to take on the energy of the environment. You thrive in places where you can utilize your intuition and where it is needed to help people feel safe and open up. You can also sense when someone needs help, and you are good at sensing when someone has the needs that they are not vocalizing. Helping professions and arts are ideal for Empaths, while others may require some adjustments to prevent overwhelm and burnout

Which Jobs to Avoid

Avoid draining jobs like sales or corporate surroundings. Dealing with needy people can be too much because customers get angry. You can pick this up, which can end up feeling overwhelming. Having to deal with people and long hours causes anxiety to many, and it might even take on a clinical form. Because you are genuine, you may not be a good pick for spots where you need to engage and convince people into arguments that aren't necessarily true and lack deep purpose. While teaching can be rewarding, it might also be overwhelming because of the noise and increased emotional and physical needs of children.

Corporate work may likewise not be right for you as this type of work relies on numbers rather than human relationship and substantial things. You won't encounter a lot of spirituality in a corporate environment, and being around competitive colleagues might not be the most suitable option for you. Noisy environments, like traffic jobs, may not be the best for you either. If you work in a place where you are regularly exposed and in need to respond to the people, you can practice many techniques to clear the negativity. Create a sense of positivity for yourself.

Working in helping professions, like medicine and teaching, is highly rewarding for Empaths. You find gratification but also burn out due to so much compassion. If you over give, you might drain yourself and end up in harm. You also take it very personally when their efforts aren't being fruitful.

Avoiding To Overbook

Never neglect the self-care to avoid burning out. While you want to heal, you also need to protect your own energy. Make sure to keep your schedule optimally full to avoid being overwhelmed.

Here are useful tips for preserving your energy at work:

- Avoid burnout and compassion fatigue
- Take regular breaks to rest and meditate
- Don't overschedule and overbook. Limit the number of your appointments to what feels right.

- Don't squeeze in appointments when you are too busy.
- Eat well and stay high in protein.
- Reduce junk foods as they highly affect your energy and mood.
- Eat antioxidants.

There is always something you can do to make your workspace more serene, such as:

- Practice deep breathing.
- Fill your space with heart energy to balance yourself out. It will infuse the space with positivity. Visitors will find space to relax, which will create a cooperative atmosphere.
- Set very clear boundaries by learning how to say no.
- Shield yourself when you detect an energy vampire or any other type of negative energy.
- Use water as a detox. Shower after a long day to wash away the stress.
- Spend enough time outside. Being outside enough will replenish your energy and take your mind away from work.

Setting Energetic Barriers at Work

Establishing boundaries means not allowing anyone to affect or manipulate you. If you are giving, think about who you are, what your limitations are, and don't let others pass them. For some, there are always emergencies, and they are creating more and more drama. Only help your coworkers if someone asks for help and are willing to make changes.

You don't only receive but also send energy. You can affect the individuals and groups of people, including your work environment. Still, you need to make sure that you are protecting your own energy. Here's how you can do that:

- Creating energetic boundaries will create mental barriers. You can use sacred objects and spend as much time in new areas as possible.
- You can visualize protective fields to create protection you can rely on.
- You can shield from the energies that are close to you to minimize the contagion.

Chapter 16: Managing Your Ability

Throughout this book, you've learned that the true self-care, and thoughtful lifestyle adjustments, can help an empath regain their health and hone their abilities. This chapter will offer the most beneficial exercises for you to practice regularly to remain grounded, center your energy, and balance your feelings.

Devote Time in Nature

Most Empaths feel a bond with the nature around them. While some have a stronger relationship with animals, others feel connected to plants and/or natural elements. Most Empaths share the love for animals and nature. You're sensitive to the pain of flora and fauna and take the matters of animal rights and environmental preservation to heart.

Empaths often love animals and nature as they pick up on the energy that the world sends out. Plants can give energy and healing. You can perceive the energy of the plants, which feels relaxing and restoring. You look upon nature with love and respect, including animals. Devoting enough time in nature helps you relax, and take it easy after a long day. It clears all of the negativity that might have surrounded your energy field.

Grounding and earthing can help you when you are feeling overstimulated or anxious. You will need to take some quiet time to recharge and release the stress. Make sure to turn off all of your electronics and fully relax. Focus on feeling calm. Relax all muscles inside your body. Let your thoughts go and don't attach to them. Visualize a tree extending down your body from top to bottom. Focus on feeling the power and energy of this tree. Imagine it rooting into the ground and giving you a sense of strength and support. When you feel anxious or afraid, think about these roots and how they are nurturing and taking care of you. Preserve this sensation of grounding when you open your eyes, knowing that this protection is always present.

Grounding will help you feel healthy and focus on your body instead of your fears. In addition to meditating, foot massages are an excellent way to relax and center your energy.

It might be painful for you to experience the increased sensitivity to physical stimuli. Whether it is smells, touch, or noises, learning how to block out the excess will help you build a strong defense. What can you do about your sensitivities? As an empath, the two extreme responses are to withdraw or to allow the stimuli which affect your mind and health. What you are aiming to do is to balance out the exposure to the overwhelming stimuli. No to remove it altogether. Your neurological structure might be more receptive to these stimuli, but it couldn't be further from the truth that you're powerless about it.

Short walks in nature or a weekend getaway to the nearest resort will help you relieve the ailments of the overload and gain the balance back. You should practice as to not go to the extremes. From being extremely outdoor to being extremely withdrawn, those are the ends of the spectrum that are making life more difficult for you. You should follow your intuition when deciding what the best choice is for you, and balance well between the rest and the activity to become more resilient.

Establish Actual or Imaginary Distance from Negativity

Visualizing a shield is helpful to many Empaths who wish to prevent overload. While meditating, try to imagine having a protective shield that filters out everything coming from the environment. This is an exceptional way to avoid the toxic energy from reaching you, and it is also a technique that you can use in everyday experiences. When you encounter a person or a situation that feels overwhelming, visualizing a shield that protects you from their influence is an excellent way to distance yourself from their toxic energy. You can use this method anywhere you are and whatever you're doing.

The principal purpose of the visualization and the way it works mentally is quite simple. Simply acknowledge that there are influences that you don't want to take in. Decide to love and care for your body in the present time instead of giving in to the others' negative energy is what gives you the power. Now, as humans and particularly this stands for Empaths, the visualization is the technique to picture these self-loving thoughts for yourself genuinely.

Examine Your Emotions

Giving your own emotional life due attention is crucial for all Empaths. Daily, make sure to work through your feelings. Distinguish those that are your own, and from those that you've collected from others.

Also, Empaths are extra sensitive to others' physical symptoms and overall wellbeing, and examining their feelings of duty toward others can be profoundly liberating.

If you're a physical empath, you'll have to learn to not only distinguish others' physical aches from your own but learn how to create boundaries. Take control over whether, and when, will you choose to allow the persons' physical sensations to be on your radar. In addition to this, examining your emotions could help you pinpoint why precisely are you choosing to take on the particular person's ailment, and why that specific pain. By examining the thought process behind the need to take in the pain of others, you will discover, and be able to surpass, the untruthful beliefs. That you must sacrifice to make others feel better or that you're responsible for others' health.

On the other hand, emotional Empaths are sensitive to others' feelings and can absorb them like a sponge, feeling others' emotions like their own. If you are this type of an empath, your main struggle will be to learn how to distinguish your feelings from those of another person. Daily reflection on your feelings will sharpen your ability to recognize the source of your emotions and be able to process them healthily.

Plan Alone Time for Yourself

Despite the type of sensitivity that you possess, you could be both introverted and extroverted in terms of sociability. This doesn't imply that you should restrain from putting in some quiet, alone time. One of the biggest misconceptions about Empaths is that they are introverts. Even though you might have little to no interest in small talk and the need to be independent in your social life, that doesn't have to mean that you are an introvert. As an empath, you relax, ground, replenish, and heal in solitude. You recharge your energy from the energetic overwhelm by being alone.

Your natural tendency to seek for the meaning in life also entails being more interested in meaningful activities rather than mundane. You likely prefer staying in and reading over going out. This is not because you don't like people and you aren't sociable, but because reading is simply a more meaningful activity for you. If you feel like choosing to stay in over going out, feel free to do so. What's making you shy away from gatherings isn't your lack of love for people, but the overwhelm of stimuli. You are more sensitive than most people to sounds, conversations, verbal and non-verbal signals, smells, and tastes. Being in a large group of people can understandably be overwhelming. By taking time to yourself, you will heal from that overwhelm, rest, and recover.

While you shouldn't blame yourself for the lack of sociability, set a goal to gradually and patiently learn to become resilient to the stimuli instead of avoiding it altogether. You will do this by balancing your activities with sufficient alone time is all right. However, keep in mind to not isolate yourself completely because isolation could lead to depression and negative self-talk. Furthermore, the lack of human-to-human relationships in your life could make you feel lonely and unlovable. It might cause you to feel like you can't establish a meaningful connection. For this reason, taking sufficient, but not too much, alone time every day, will gradually enforce and strengthen your ability to filter rather than pull back and avoid exposure entirely.

The final chapter of this book provided you with useful guidance to manage your empathic abilities. While most people benefit from rest, leisure, and entertainment, you recharge in seclusion and from the connection that you share with the spiritual. From staying in tune with nature to spending enough time in lonely self-reflection, it is the care for your inner being that will enforce you to thrive as an empath. Make sure to give the inner self enough attention as you will be rewarded with a sense of inner peace and a balanced, centered mind.

Conclusion

Congratulations! You've come to the end of the journey to understanding empathy. This book served to give detailed explanations of empathy and the unique traits that make an empath special.

In this book, you've learned that being an empath is more than being sensitive. While being an empath means that you have the possibility to identify subtle irregularities in your surroundings, as well as sense others' hidden emotions, it doesn't mean that you are simply a passive energetic sponge. This book has presented you with the detailed breakdown of the Empaths' unique traits, but it also showed you the right steps you can take to shift your mindset and move toward empowerment. By offering insight into the forms of empathy and the levels of empathic development, this book has provided you with a guide to track your own progress and reveal the necessary steps in order to grow.

By highlighting success and empowerment, this book has taught you that sensitivities and kindness are not weaknesses. By using the right techniques, you can train your mind to use understanding, compassion, and vulnerability to power through life. Unlike most people, your spiritual sensitivities won't allow you to grow and progress on aggression, speed, and productivity. Instead, what this book has hopefully taught you is that the way to a successful, meaningful life for an empath is to look within and immerse yourself into the positivity, love, and acceptance.

Still, being an empath means having to overcome numerous challenges in your daily life. From the relationship with your parents, to work, and romantic relationship, a path for an empath to grow is to set boundaries and nurture their own, authentic self. Hopefully, this book has provided you with sufficient strategies to not only understand but also be willing to fully accept and love your true self.

Last, but not least, this book has provided you with instructions to protect your own health and energy every step of the way. From healing headaches to preserving your inner peace in the midst of conflict, this book has shed light on many topics that Empaths find hard to handle. While empathic development means growing your sensitivity, resilience, consciousness, and spiritual strength, staying in control will require constant work on grounding, balance and centering. This book will come in handy to navigate your newfound freedom and talents, as you journey from becoming aware that you are an empath, to becoming a fully mature, authentic self.

Bibliography

Acevedo, B. P., Aron, E. N., Aron, A., Sangster, M. D., Collins, N., & Brown, L. L. (2014). The highly sensitive brain: an fMRI study of sensory processing sensitivity and response to others' emotions. Brain and behavior, 4(4), 580-594.

Aron, E. N., & Aron, A. (1997). Sensory-processing sensitivity and its relation to introversion and emotionality. Journal of personality and social psychology, 73(2), 345.

Campion, L. (2018). The Art of Psychic Reiki: Developing Your Intuitive and Empathic Abilities for Energy Healing. New Harbinger Publications.

Dunn, W. (1997). The impact of sensory processing abilities on the daily lives of young children and their families: A conceptual model. Infants and young children, 9, 23-35.

Greiner, J. (2018). Empath: Understanding Your Gift, Protecting your Energy and Finding Peace in a Chaotic World. Jessica Greiner.

Liss, M., Timmel, L., Baxley, K., & Killingsworth, P. (2005). Sensory processing sensitivity and its relation to parental bonding, anxiety, and depression. Personality and individual differences, 39(8), 1429-1439.

Loggia, M. L., Mogil, J. S., & Bushnell, M. C. (2008). Empathy hurts: compassion for another increases both sensory and affective components of pain perception. Pain, 136(1-2), 168-176.

Mason, R. (2005). The Energy Psychiatry of Judith Orloff, MD. Alternative & Complementary Therapies, 11(1), 32-36.

Orloff, J. (2017). The Empath's Survival Guide: Life Strategies for Sensitive People. Sounds True.

Tajadura-Jiménez, A., & Tsakiris, M. (2014). Balancing the "inner" and the "outer" self: Interoceptive sensitivity modulates self–other boundaries. Journal of Experimental Psychology: General, 143(2), 736.

About the Author

Monique Joiner Siedlak is a writer, witch, and warrior on a mission to awaken people to their greatest potential through the power of storytelling infused with mysticism, modern paganism, and new age spirituality. At the young age of 12, she began rigorously studying the fascinating philosophy of Wicca. By the time she was 20, she was self-initiated into the craft, and hasn't looked back ever since. To this day, she has authored over 35 books pertaining to the magick and mysteries of life.

Originally from Long Island, New York, Monique is now a proud inhabitant of Northeast Florida; however, she considers herself to be a citizen of Mother Earth. When she doesn't have a book or pen in hand, she loves exploring new places and learning new things. And being the nature lover that she is, she considers herself to be an avid animal advocate.

To find out more about Monique Joiner Siedlak artistically, spiritually, and personally, feel free to visit her official **website**.

More Books by Monique Joiner Siedlak

African Magic

Hoodoo

Seven African Powers: The Orishas

Cooking For the Orishas

Lucumi: The Ways of Santeria

Voodoo of Louisiana

The Yoga Collective

Yoga for Beginners

Yoga for Stress

Yoga for Back Pain

Yoga for Weight Loss

Yoga for Flexibility

Yoga for Advanced Beginners

Yoga for Fitness

Yoga for Runners

Yoga for Energy

Yoga for Your Sex Life

Yoga to Beat Depression and Anxiety

Yoga for Menstruation

Yoga to Detox Your Body

Toga to Tone Your Body

A Natural Beautiful You

Creating Your Own Body Butter

Creating Your Own Body Scrub

Creating Your Own Body Spray